WITHDRAWN

WITHDRAWN

THE FAT RADISH KITCHEN DIARIES

BEN TOWILL + PHIL WINSER + NICK WILBER WITH JULIA TURSHEN

Photographed by Nicole Franzen

RIZZOLI
NEW YORK

New York · Paris · London · Milan

To our grandparents, who taught us so much:
Bobby Winser and Polly Towill

contents

introduction

This book bears the name of our New York City restaurant, but it's more than a collection of its recipes. It's a chronicle of stories from Phil, me, and our chef, Nick; a diary of meals we created together; beloved dishes from our childhoods; and experiences where a dish or an ingredient had been the very thing that made the moment so memorable. For us, there is nothing more exciting than the anticipation of the seasons and cooking within them. (What a pretentious thing to say, but we promise it's true.)

Before the age of sixteen, I hadn't thought about food in any great detail. I certainly appreciated great food, but it wasn't until I suffered from chronic fatigue that food came into focus. I spent that year in bed sleeping for up to twenty hours a day. With no magical pill to cure me, I looked at alternative ways to get back on my feet. With the support of some forward-thinking friends and family, I began healing myself through diet. The results were amazing: my energy levels increased, and all the symptoms gradually subsided. It was a eureka moment, which seems so obvious now—you are what you eat. This, in essence, is where the philosophy for the restaurant began. Armed once again with bags of energy and a burning desire to learn about food, I began working for great chefs, who taught me about respecting ingredients and the work that went into producing them. I cooked my way from Oxford to Cornwall via London and then landed in New York.

Phil and I have been friends since childhood and I have loved watching his creative process since we were kids. (When most teenage boys were throwing their clothes on the floor, Phil was designing a hanging wardrobe on a pulley system above his bed.) In April 2007, I got an email saying that said he would be coming through New York after traveling the world. Phil arrived one summer evening in the middle of dinner service at the restaurant I was working in with his old leather suitcases under his arms. (They are called "backpackers" for a reason, but not Mr. Winser, who was traveling with his grandfather's luggage.) His one-week stay turned into three months, which has turned into seven years, three restaurants, a catering and events company, and some truly magical memories. Phil's love of travel and ability to translate his experiences into design blows me away. Phil also might be one of the most passionate, if not the tidiest, home cooks I have ever met. His Nearly World-Famous Potato Salad speaks for itself.

Nick's introduction to the Radish began with a poorly written Craigslist post by yours truly. When this all-American gentleman in a trucker hat showed up, we knew we had our chef. I am sure that while growing up in Colorado, Nick never thought that he would be subjected to so many English dishes, but he has embraced every last one (even the Scotch Egg) and somehow improved them. When he created the Celery Root Pot Pie, my eyes did the same thing they do, I will unabashedly admit, when watching *Love Actually* on Christmas Day. (For those who have not watched this film, please stop reading and do so at once.)

We highly recommend cooking a whole fish on the beach next summer, and making a complete roast on a Sunday during the fall (hopefully with a Hawaiian shirt on and a few glasses of wine). Be sure to make a beet crumble at Thanksgiving, because even though your family might gasp at the description, they will love the taste and claim it as a family tradition. Impress guests at your next (or first) dinner party with Monkfish Vindaloo; it works every time. Or in true Fat Radish style, collect all the vegetables you can find and make the Fat Radish Plate, and watch even your most manly guests eat every last green leaf.

We hope that you have as much fun working your way through the recipes, and making them your own, as we did getting them down on paper.

Enjoy,

Ben & Phil

This page: Phil discusses the night's specials with the kitchen team. Opposite page: We found the restaurant's big red R in a flea market just before we opened the doors. Nick—and his signature trucker hat—in the kitchen.

SPRING

STEWED RHUBARB WITH YOGURT

Stewed fruit, particularly plums and rhubarb, is a big thing in England. It's always in the fridge. When we cooked at Ben's mom's bed and breakfast, we often served it to guests at breakfast time.

Serves 8

1½ cups sugar
1 orange, halved
1 star anise
A dozen allspice berries
2 bay leaves
1 small cinnamon stick
Pinch salt
1½ pounds rhubarb, trimmed and cut crosswise into 2-inch pieces
   (about 4½ cups)
Plain yogurt for serving
Chopped, toasted almonds for serving

Combine the sugar, orange halves, star anise, allspice, bay leaves, cinnamon and salt together in a large saucepan with 1½ cups water. Bring to a boil over high heat, stirring the sugar until it dissolves. Lower the heat to medium, add the rhubarb, and simmer until the rhubarb is just tender, about 10 minutes. Take the pan off of the heat and allow the rhubarb to cool in the liquid until it's room temperature. Discard the star anise, allspice, and cinnamon stick.

To serve, place ½ cup of the poached rhubarb along with a large spoonful of its poaching liquid on top of yogurt and sprinkle with some toasted almonds. Extra rhubarb can be stored in its poaching liquid in the fridge for 3–4 days.

KALE + GOAT CHEESE MUFFINS

We ran the restaurant at Ruschmeyer's Hotel in Montauk for two summers and part of the deal was preparing a continental buffet for the hotel guests. These muffins were a staple for the active, health-conscious guests.

Makes 12 muffins

2 tablespoons butter, plus extra for the tin
2 cups milk
½ pound kale, roughly chopped
2 eggs
2 teaspoons baking soda
2 teaspoons baking powder
1 teaspoon salt
A pinch of cayenne
2 cups flour
¼ cup soft goat cheese
¼ cup coarsely grated Parmesan

Preheat oven to 350°F and butter a standard 12-cup muffin tin or line it with paper liners. Set the tin aside.

Meanwhile, place the 2 tablespoons of butter in a medium pot set over medium heat along with the milk. Once the mixture comes barely to a boil, add the kale and turn the heat down. Simmer until the kale is totally softened, about 5 minutes. Place the mixture in a food processor or blender and puree (always be careful when pureeing hot liquids and place a kitchen towel on top of the lid). Set the mixture aside to cool.

Once cool, place the kale mixture into a large bowl and whisk in the eggs, baking soda, baking powder, salt, and cayenne. Stir in the flour. Fill the muffin cups halfway with half of the batter. Evenly divide the goat cheese among the muffins and then top each bit of goat cheese with the rest of the muffin batter. Top each muffin with a bit of Parmesan.

Place the tin in the oven and bake until the muffins are risen, browned, and firm to the touch, about 25 minutes.

Let the muffins cool before serving.

BIRCHERS MUESLI

Muesli is a nice warm-weather alternative to oatmeal. We used to make it a lot when we were catering since the base is something you can make in advance, and it's even better if you do. The key is to add the grated apples and pears at the last minute so that they don't go brown.

Serves 6

2 cups rolled oats
3 cups pear juice or apple juice
1 each green apple and pear, coarsely grated (don't bother peeling, just
   discard the cores and seeds)
1½ cups plain yogurt
¼ cup roughly chopped, toasted pistachios
Berries, fresh currants (if you can find them), and fresh mint for serving

Place the oats in a large bowl and pour the pear juice over them. Let mixture sit for at least an hour at room temperature or overnight in the refrigerator. Just before serving, stir in the apples, pears, yogurt, and pistachios. Serve with plenty of berries and currants and a few bits of torn mint.

SWEET PEA POT PIE

We were chatting with our chef Nick, a.k.a. "The Pie King," about doing a take on chicken pot pie that was more vegetable-driven. He came up with the Celery Root Pot Pie (see page 180) for the winter and now we put a different one on the menu each season. Our sweet pea version is a staple of the springtime menu.

Serves 4

Coarse salt
4 cups shelled fresh English peas
1 cup each snow peas and snap peas, trimmed and halved crosswise
2 tablespoons olive oil
½ large yellow onion, finely diced
1 cup low-sodium vegetable stock
3 tablespoons unsalted butter
2 tablespoons sherry vinegar
2 tablespoons chopped mint
Freshly ground black pepper
2 egg yolks, beaten together
1 large sheet puff pastry

Bring a large pot of salted water to a boil. Add 1 cup of the English peas and the snow and snap peas. Cook until the vegetables are tender and green, about 2 minutes. Drain the vegetables, rinse them with cold water, and set them aside in a large bowl.

Place the olive oil in a large saucepan set over medium heat. Add the onions and cook until they're soft, about 10 minutes. Add the vegetable stock and bring the mixture to a boil. Add the remaining 3 cups of English peas and cook until they're just tender, 2 minutes. Place the mixture into a blender and blend until smooth. Add the butter and vinegar and blend until super smooth.

Pour the puree over the reserved English, snow, and snap peas. Stir in the mint and season the mixture to taste with salt and pepper.

Transfer the mixture to a large baking dish (or 4 individual baking dishes) and brush the exterior rim with the egg yolk. Cut the pastry to fit, allowing for about an inch of overhang from the edge, and drape over the top of the baking dish, pressing it to the sides to adhere with the egg yolk. Brush the top with the remaining egg yolk. Refrigerate the pie for at least 30 minutes to allow the egg yolk to form a seal with the puff pastry.

Bake at 375°F until golden brown, 20 minutes. Serve hot.

ASPARAGUS + BACON SALAD

In our opinion, if you're going to put croutons in a salad, they should be awesome. Otherwise, they're just dry, bummer pieces of bread. This salad is all about the croutons and giving them love. Be sure to tear the bread so that the croutons are rough and have all sorts of uneven edges that can soak up the bacon fat.

Serves 4

3 tablespoons freshly squeezed lemon juice
1 tablespoon Dijon mustard
½ cup extra virgin olive oil
Coarse salt and freshly ground black pepper
1 large bunch asparagus, tough ends discarded, cut into bite-sized pieces
¾ pound unsliced smoked bacon, cut into bite-sized pieces
4 thick slices country bread, crusts removed, torn into large chunks
One 6-inch sprig rosemary, leaves removed from stem, stem discarded
1 large garlic clove, thinly sliced
Small handful parsley leaves

In a small bowl, whisk together the lemon juice, mustard, and olive oil. Season to taste with salt and pepper and set the dressing aside.

Bring a large pot of water to a boil and salt it generously. Add the asparagus and cook until just-tender and bright green, about 2–3 minutes. Immediately transfer the asparagus to an ice bath to stop it from cooking. Drain it, place it in a large bowl and set it aside.

Meanwhile, place the bacon in a heavy skillet set over medium heat and cook, stirring now and then, until it's crisp and all the fat has rendered off. Using a slotted spoon, transfer the bacon from the pan to a paper towel lined plate and set it aside, being sure to leave the fat in the pan and the flame on.

Add the bread, rosemary, and garlic to the pan. Toss to combine all of those lovely things with all of the even more lovely bacon fat. Cook, stirring, until the croutons are brown and crisp, about 4 minutes.

Add the bacon to the reserved asparagus along with the parsley and the warm croutons. Toss with the reserved dressing and serve immediately.

PHIL'S NEARLY WORLD-FAMOUS NEW POTATO SALAD

PHIL: Everyone asks me to make this.
BEN: Do they?
PHIL: They do. You know, it's in my nearly world-famous arsenal. I'm not normally
        a one-trick pony, but when it comes to potato salad, I am.
BEN: What are people's reactions?
PHIL: "I need the recipe!"
BEN: Tell them to buy the book.

Serves 6

Coarse salt
1½ pounds new potatoes
½ pound green beans
1 tablespoon whole grain mustard
1 tablespoon Dijon mustard
1 tablespoon white wine vinegar
¼ cup mayonnaise or creme fraîche
3 Six-Minute Eggs (see page 68), peeled
¼ cup Pickled Red Onions, drained
A large handful roughly chopped leafy herbs (a mix of dill,
   chives, and parsley is nice)
Freshly ground black pepper

Bring a large pot of water to a boil and season with salt. Add the potatoes and cook until just tender, about 20 minutes. Use a slotted spoon to transfer the potatoes to a bowl. When they're barely cool enough to handle, slice each potato in half. Add the green beans to the pot and cook until just tender, about 2 minutes. Drain them and transfer to the bowl with the potatoes.

Meanwhile, whisk together the mustards and vinegar with the mayonnaise or creme fraîche in a small bowl. Pour the mixture over the potatoes and beans and stir to combine. Break in the eggs with your hands and scatter in the onions and herbs. Gently stir everything together. Season to taste with more salt and pepper and serve immediately.

PICKLED RED ONIONS

In addition to spiking potato salad, these onions are great served alongside cheese or on sandwiches. These can be kept in an airtight jar in the fridge for up to a month.

Makes 1 pint

2 tablespoons olive oil
2 red onions, thinly sliced
1 teaspoon coarse salt
½ cup red wine or sherry vinegar

Place the olive oil in a large skillet set over very high heat. When the oil just begins to smoke, add the onions to the pan. Cook, stirring now and then, until they begin to char in spots, about 5 minutes. Sprinkle with the salt and pour the vinegar over the onions. Turn off the heat immediately. Transfer the onions and all of the vinegar to a jar or a bowl and add ½ cup water. Allow the onions to sit at room temperature for at least an hour before serving.

GRILLED SPRING CABBAGE | WHITE BEAN SOUP

We made this for a staff lunch one day and thought, "this has to be on the menu." Grilling the cabbage before adding it to the broth gives this homey yet impressive soup a tremendous depth of smoky flavor. Note that this soup is an excellent place to put your leftover Parmesan rinds! They also add great flavor.

Serves 8

½ head Savoy cabbage (about a pound), cut into 4 wedges
Olive oil
Coarse salt
Freshly ground black pepper
2 yellow onions, finely diced
1 carrot, peeled and finely diced
2 celery stalks, finely diced
2 cups dry white beans, soaked in cold water overnight and drained
1 small piece Parmesan rind
Zest from 1 lemon
Grated Parmesan for serving

Preheat grill or grill pan on high so the heat is super hot. Rub each cabbage wedge with a tablespoon of olive oil and plenty of salt and pepper. Grill them until charred all over, about 1–2 minutes per side. Remove them from the grill and allow to cool. Roughly chop each wedge, discarding the tough bits of core, and set the cabbage aside.

Meanwhile, heat a few tablespoons of olive oil in a large soup pot set over medium heat. Add the onions, carrot, and celery and cook, stirring now and then, until softened, about 10 minutes. Add the drained beans, the Parmesan rind, and the reserved cabbage. Add 6 cups of cold water, bring the soup to a boil, and then lower the heat and partially cover the pot. Allow the soup to simmer, stirring it every so often, until the beans are soft, about 1–2 hours.

Remove and discard the Parmesan rind and season the soup with salt and pepper to taste. Stir in the lemon zest and serve the soup hot with grated Parmesan on each portion.

MISO-GLAZED TURNIPS

This is our version of miso-glazed black cod: vegetable, take the focus. Serve with some of the spicy, raw greens from the tops of the turnips and a few slices of raw turnip, too.

Serves 4

¼ cup mirin
¼ cup sake or dry vermouth
½ cup sweet white miso paste
½ cup sugar
½ cup vegetable stock (or water)
2 pounds turnips, peeled and roughly chopped

Whisk together the mirin, sake, miso, and sugar in a large skillet set over high heat. Bring to a boil. Turn the heat to low and simmer until the sauce is thick and a bit glossy, about 10 minutes. Whisk in the vegetable stock (or water) and add the turnips to the skillet. Bring the mixture back to a boil and lower the heat once again. Simmer until the turnips are tender, about 20 minutes. Serve hot or at room temperature.

SUNDAY NIGHT PEA + SPICY SAUSAGE PASTA

PHIL: My dear friend Richard and I used to work together at a catering company in London. On Sundays, we would spend all of our money to make this dish. We were obsessed with the idea of reducing things, so we'd let the sauce simmer for hours. Sometimes dinner wasn't ready until two in the morning, and the friends we'd invited were long gone. When I came to the US and learned about cooking with spicy sausage, I realized it was possible to get great flavor without spending all day leaning over a pot.

Serves 6–8

2 tablespoons olive oil
1 large yellow onion, thinly sliced
8 garlic cloves, finely chopped
1 dried bay leaf
2 sprigs fresh thyme
Coarse salt
½ teaspoon dried Italian herb mix (oregano, basil, rosemary, etc.)
¾ pound spicy pork sausage, meat removed from casings (discard casings)
1 (28-ounce) can diced tomatoes (preferably San Marzano)
3 tablespoons heavy cream
1 cup frozen peas
1 pound rigatoni pasta, cooked in salted water until al dente
Freshly grated Parmesan for serving

Place the olive oil in a heavy pot set over medium heat. Add the onion, garlic, bay leaf, thyme, and a big pinch of salt. Cook, stirring now and then, until softened, 10 minutes. Push the onions to the side and add the dry herb mix to the middle of the pot and stir so that it can get a little toasty, about 30 seconds. Stir the herbs thoroughly into the onions. Add the sausage, turn the heat up to high and cook, stirring to break up the meat, until the sausage is crumbly and a bit browned, 10 minutes. Stir in the tomatoes and all of their juice and bring the mixture to a boil. Lower the heat and allow the sauce to simmer, stirring now and then, until it's a bit reduced, about 30 minutes. Add the cream and peas to the pot and stir just to combine and until the peas are just defrosted, about a minute. Season the sauce with salt and toss with the just-cooked rigatoni. Serve with plenty of freshly grated Parmesan.

BROCCOLI RABE PASTA WITH GREAT BREADCRUMBS

When our chef Nick was working at an Italian restaurant, he had a coworker named Fabio who would make a version of this for family meal. It was something Fabio's mother made often in her home region of Puglia, Italy. Broccoli rabe is best in spring because once it's been "wintered over" (farmer talk for surviving the winter), it gets wonderfully sweet.

Serves 8

6 garlic cloves, very thinly sliced
1 teaspoon red chili flakes
8 anchovy filets
¾ cup extra virgin olive oil
Coarse salt
1 large bunch broccoli rabe, tough stem ends removed and discarded,
    roughly chopped
1 cup breadcrumbs
½ cup sundried tomatoes, finely chopped
2 tablespoons finely chopped fresh parsley
1 pound orecchiette (or any pasta shape you like)

Place the garlic, chili flakes, anchovies, and olive oil in a large skillet over low heat. Cook the mixture, stirring now and then, until the anchovies are completely dissolved and the garlic is totally transparent, about 20 minutes. Keep the heat nice and low so that the garlic doesn't take on any color. You just want it to surrender and release all of its sweetness into the oil. Remove the mixture from the heat and set it aside.

Meanwhile, bring a large pot of water to a boil and salt it liberally. Place the broccoli rabe in the boiling water and cook until it's bright green, about 3 minutes. Using a handheld strainer, transfer the broccoli rabe to a colander and rinse it immediately with cold water. Squeeze the broccoli rabe dry and transfer it to a food processor. Pulse to roughly chop it and, while the machine is running, slowly drizzle in ½ cup of the olive oil mixture, being sure to get some of the anchovies and garlic in, too. Process until everything is just smooth and combined, but not too smooth. A little texture is nice. Season the sauce to taste with salt and set aside.

Meanwhile, place the skillet with the remaining ¼ cup of the olive oil mixture back on the stove over medium heat. Add the breadcrumbs and the sundried tomatoes, and cook, stirring now and then, until the breadcrumbs are crisp, about 5–10 minutes. Turn off the heat, stir in the parsley, and set the breadcrumbs aside.

To finish the dish, bring the pot of water back to a boil and add the pasta. Cook until just al dente. Drain the pasta, return it to the pot, and stir in the broccoli rabe sauce. Transfer the pasta to a serving bowl and scatter with the breadcrumbs. Serve immediately.

NOTE: Any extra breadcrumbs are delicious on salad (such as the Kale Caesar on page 178) or scatter them on roasted tomatoes, roasted cauliflower, or grilled asparagus for an easy side dish.

TROUT WITH CITRUS + CHAMOMILE DRESSING

Our chef Nick picked up some fresh chamomile at the market one day and we got to talking about how to use it as an herb for cooking. We found that its floral flavor is such a nice match for the earthy taste of fresh-water fish, like trout. We normally serve this dish with Greens, Garlic + Grains (see page 62).

Serves 4

4 tablespoons unsalted butter
1½ tablespoons dry chamomile flowers (source at your local farmers'
  market or use the contents of 2 chamomile tea bags)
Coarse salt
2 tablespoons extra virgin olive oil
4 skin-on trout fillets, patted dry with paper towels
Coarse salt
Segments from a Meyer lemon (or a regular lemon)*
2 tablespoons pine nuts, lightly toasted

Place the butter, chamomile, and a pinch of coarse salt in a small saucepan set over low heat. Cook the mixture until the chamomile aroma is really strong and fully steeped (be careful not to brown it), about 5 minutes. Strain the butter into a bowl, discarding the chamomile, and set aside.

Place the olive oil in a large nonstick skillet set over high heat. Carefully place the trout filets, skin side down, in the pan in an even, single layer (do this in batches if necessary, depending on the size of your pan). Sprinkle the tops of the filets with a good bit of salt. Turn the heat down to medium and cook until the skin is crispy, about 3 minutes. Carefully turn the fillets over. Pour in the reserved chamomile butter and scatter the lemon segments and pine nuts over the fish. Turn off the heat and allow the fish to sit in the pan until the residual heat cooks it through, about 2 more minutes.

Transfer the fish to plates, being sure to get plenty of the butter and some bits of lemon and pine nuts over each portion.

*HOW TO SEGMENT A LEMON
Use your paring knife to remove the skin and pith from the fruit. Hold the peeled lemon in your hand and carefully insert your knife between two segments, freeing the wedges of fruit from the thin membranes that hold them in place.

SPRING ONION RINGS WITH TARTAR SAUCE

This recipe comes from Ben's brother Alexander who has a burger restaurant in Cornwall, England called The Hub. He is basically the Cornish Burger King. We love making these with huge spring onions, but you can use regular yellow onions. The tartar sauce is also lovely on fried or roasted fish or chicken.

Serves 4

½ cup mayonnaise
1 tablespoon whole grain mustard
1 tablespoon capers
3 cornichons, finely diced
1 tablespoon chopped fresh dill
1 teaspoon chopped fresh tarragon
Coarse salt
2 cups flour, divided
½ cup cornstarch
1 teaspoon freshly ground black pepper
2 cups sparkling water
Vegetable oil for frying
6 very large spring onions, cut into thick slices and separated into rings

In a small bowl, stir together the mayonnaise, mustard, capers, cornichons, dill, and tarragon and season to taste with salt. Set the tartar sauce aside.

Place 1 cup of flour into a mixing bowl and set aside.

Place the other cup of flour in another bowl, and whisk in the cornstarch, a teaspoon of salt, and pepper. Whisk in the sparkling water.

Heat up a few inches of oil in a large, heavy pot. Line a baking sheet with paper towels and set aside.

Place the onions in the plain flour and toss to combine. Working with one onion ring at a time, tap the excess flour off of the onions and then dip them into the batter, letting the excess drip off. Use tongs to place them into the hot oil. Fry, turning once or twice, until browned all over and crisp, about 4 minutes. Transfer the onions rings to the prepared baking sheet and continue frying until you've used up all of your onions and batter. Sprinkle the onion rings with salt and serve immediately with the tartar sauce.

Mornings at the market – the best part of the day

This page, clockwise from top left: At the Greenmarket with Julia, our fearless writer. The Union Square Greenmarket in full swing. Bok choi for Greens, Garlic and Grains. **Opposite page, from top left:** Beautiful herbs, destined for the Radish. Ben Shaw, the owner of Garden of Spices Farm, which provides the eggs for the restaurant. Nevia No, the founder of Bhodi Tree Farms, and Debbie Farmer at their stand. (The farm's slogan is "veggies with spirit".) Mixed radishes, which we serve with olive tapenade instead of bread.

CHARRED SNAP PEAS WITH MINT SALT + CHILI OIL

This is a cool, clever thing to make when people come over for drinks or to serve before dinner. Sometimes we do this with fresh English peas, too. If you don't want to go to the trouble of making the chili oil or mint salt, simply sprinkle some salt, chili flakes, or torn mint leaves (or a combination of the three) over the peas.

Serves 4

2 tablespoons mint leaves
1 teaspoon coarse salt
Pinch red chili flakes
3 tablespoons olive oil, divided
1 pound fresh snap peas

Grind the mint and salt together either in a mortar and pestle or in a food processor. Set the mint salt aside.

Combine the chili flakes and 2 tablespoons of the olive oil in a cast iron pan set over medium heat. Warm the mixture until the chili flakes just start to sizzle. Transfer the oil to a bowl and set it aside.

Return the pan to the heat and turn it up to high. Add the snap peas and the remaining tablespoon of olive oil. Cook, stirring the snap peas a bit, until they're charred in places, about 1–2 minutes. Serve immediately, drizzled with the chili oil and sprinkled with the mint salt.

BROWN RICE KEDGEREE

PHIL: I used to have this every Christmas Eve back in England with my family. Now that I'm rarely back home over the holidays, I carry on the tradition in New York and make it for my loved ones here.

Serves 4

¼ cup creme fraîche
Zest and juice of 1 lime
Pinch of cayenne pepper
2 tablespoons unsalted butter
1 yellow onion, finely diced
5 cardamom pods
1 teaspoon ground turmeric
2 teaspoons ground cumin
2 teaspoons ground coriander
1 cup brown basmati rice
Coarse salt
½ pound smoked haddock
½ teaspoon freshly ground black pepper
2 bay leaves
1 cup heavy cream
1 cup frozen peas, defrosted
3 Six-Minute Eggs (see page 68), quartered
Small handful chopped chives and chive flowers

In a small bowl, whisk together the creme fraîche with the lime zest, juice and cayenne. Set the mixture aside while you prepare the kedgeree.

Melt the butter in a large pot set over medium heat and add the onion, cardamom, turmeric, cumin, coriander, and a teaspoon of salt. Cook, stirring now and then, until the onions are softened, about 10 minutes. Add the rice along with 1¾ cups cold water and another large pinch of salt. Bring to a boil. Lower the heat, cover the pot, and simmer until the rice is cooked through, about 45 minutes.

Meanwhile, place the haddock in another medium pot along with the pepper, bay leaves, and cream. Simmer while the rice is cooking to infuse the cream with the haddock's flavor. Remove and discard the bay leaves and stir the haddock and the cream into the rice along with the peas. Season the kedgeree to taste with salt.

To serve, transfer the kedegree to a serving bowl or, more simply, serve it in the pot. Drizzle the reserved crème fraîche mixture over the kedegree, place the eggs on top, scatter with the chives and chive flowers, and serve immediately.

LEEK + PEEKYTOE CRAB GRATIN

This dip is like crack. If you've got a few people coming over for a cocktail, serve this for them to snack on. Really, this is how to one-up your neighbor.

Serves 8

2 tablespoons unsalted butter
2 leeks, white and light green parts only, washed and finely diced
½ cup sherry
1 cup heavy cream
1 pound cleaned crab meat (use whatever type you like)
Coarse salt and freshly ground black pepper
½ cup breadcrumbs
½ cup coarsely grated sharp white cheddar cheese
Pinch grated nutmeg
Pinch red chili flakes
2 tablespoons olive oil
Lemon wedges for serving
Toast for serving

Preheat oven to 400°F.

Place the butter in an ovenproof skillet set over medium heat. Add the leeks and cook, stirring now and then, until softened, about 10 minutes. Add the sherry, turn the heat to high and bring to a boil. Cook until the sherry is nearly evaporated, 5 minutes. Add the cream to the pan, turn the heat to low and simmer until the cream is slightly reduced, 5 minutes. Allow the cream mixture to cool. Stir the crab into the cooled cream mixture and season with salt and pepper to taste.

Meanwhile, in a small bowl, stir together the breadcrumbs, cheese, nutmeg, and chili flakes. Cover the crab mixture evenly with the breadcrumb mixture and drizzle with olive oil. Place the skillet in the oven and bake until the top is golden brown and the sides are bubbling, about 10–15 minutes. Serve hot with lemon wedges alongside and plenty of toast.

LAMB SANDWICHES FOR A CROWD

We had the pleasure of having lunch one day at the summer home of Robin Standefer and Stephen Alesch (the duo behind the design firm Roman and Williams). They were grilling lamb and, to get to the table, we had to walk through the herb garden. They encouraged us to pick herbs on our way to throw on our sandwiches. This is our version of that perfect meal.

Serves 12

Leaves from 1 bunch basil
Leaves from 1 bunch mint
Olive oil
Coarse salt
1 boneless leg of lamb (about 5 pounds), trimmed of excess fat and
  butterflied
2 pints cherry tomatoes
½ cup each finely chopped parsley, chives, and dill, plus extra for serving
4 shallots, finely chopped
¼ cup red wine vinegar
Warm pita bread for serving
Tzatziki for serving

Combine basil and mint in blender with a cup of olive oil and a teaspoon of salt. Puree until smooth. Place the lamb in a large container or plastic bag and pour the herb oil over it. Cover and marinate the lamb overnight in the refrigerator.

Preheat oven to 250°F. Bring the lamb to room temperature. Remove from bag and reserve marinade. Roll the lamb like a yoga mat. Using a few pieces of kitchen string, tie the lamb every couple of inches so it holds together.

Transfer the lamb to a roasting dish with its marinade and place the lamb in the oven. Roast, turning occasionally, until a digital thermometer registers 140°F, about 3 hours depending on the size of the lamb.

Remove the lamb from the oven and allow it to rest at least 15 minutes before carving. Thinly slice the lamb, discarding the string as you go.

Meanwhile, combine the tomatoes with the chopped herbs, ½ cup of olive oil, the shallots, and the vinegar. Season the mixture with salt to taste.

Pile the lamb in the warmed pita breads with plenty of the tomatoes and Tzatziki and serve with bowls of extra herbs so guests can add more to their sandwiches.

TZATZIKI

Makes 1 quart

1 English cucumber, ends discarded
4 garlic cloves, minced
3 cups full-fat Greek yogurt
½ cup freshly squeezed lemon juice
½ cup roughly chopped dill
Coarse salt

Coarsely grate the cucumber and place it in the center of a clean tea towel. Wrap the cucumber as you would a piece of candy and wring it over the sink so all of its liquid drains off. Place the dry cucumber in a large bowl and stir together with the garlic, yogurt, lemon juice, and dill. Season to taste with salt.

GRILLED ASPARAGUS WITH GRIBICHE AND/OR AJO BLANCO

Serve grilled asparagus with one of these sauces or offer both at the same time.
The Gribiche is a riff on the classic combination of asparagus and eggs.
The Ajo Blanco, made of almonds, offers a similar richness but is totally vegan.

Serves 6

For The Gribiche
1 cup mayonnaise
1 tablespoon whole grain mustard
Juice of ½ lemon
2 hard-boiled eggs, finely chopped
¼ cup finely chopped chives
Coarse salt and freshly ground black pepper

For The Ajo Blanco
½ cup raw almonds, soaked in water overnight and drained
6 cloves roasted garlic (see page 132)
Zest from ½ lemon
Pinch red chili flake
¼ cup olive oil
Coarse salt
A few chopped almonds for serving

For The Asparagus
2 bunches asparagus, tough ends discarded
2 tablespoons olive oil
Coarse salt
1 small handful grated Parmesan
Finely grated zest of 1 lemon

For The Gribiche, stir together all of the ingredients and season to taste with salt and pepper.

For The Ajo Blanco, place the almonds in a blender with the garlic, lemon zest, chili flakes, olive oil and ½ cup cold water. Puree until smooth and season to taste with salt. Pour into a bowl and garnish with chopped almonds.

Get your grill or grill pan going on high heat. Toss the asparagus with the olive oil and sprinkle them with a pinch of coarse salt. Grill until charred in places, 5 minutes. Remove the asparagus from the grill and scatter with the grated Parmesan and lemon zest. Serve immediately with Gribiche and/or Ajo Blanco.

MOROCCAN LEG OF LAMB WITH COUSCOUS

BEN: This is what I made for my first-ever gig when I had to cook for an enormous amount of people. A great way to serve a crowd, this recipe might appear intimidating but it couldn't be easier—it's impressive but it's not tricky. Note that if you can tie a shoelace, you can tie a leg of lamb.

Serves a crowd of about 10 impressively

1 teaspoon red chili flakes
1 teaspoon ground cayenne pepper
2 teaspoons ground caraway
2 teaspoons ground ginger
1 tablespoon ground coriander
1 tablespoon ground cumin, plus an extra tablespoon for finishing
Coarse salt
1 boneless leg of lamb (about 5 pounds), trimmed of excess fat and
   butterflied
1 cup couscous
Extra virgin olive oil
1 yellow onion, diced
3 garlic cloves, thinly sliced
Half of a fresh red chili, finely chopped
Leaves from 3 sprigs of thyme, finely chopped
2 carrots, peeled and cut into ¼-inch slices
1 bunch Swiss chard, stems thinly sliced and leaves roughly chopped
1 cup dates, pitted and roughly chopped
½ cup honey

Preheat oven to 300°F.

In a small bowl, combine all of the spices with a tablespoon of salt. Rub the spice mixture all over the lamb, inside and out. Set the lamb aside while you prepare the couscous.

spring roast

Place the couscous in a large bowl with a tablespoon of olive oil and a large pinch of salt. Stir in 1½ cups boiling water and cover the bowl tightly with plastic wrap. Once the couscous absorbs all of the water, about 10 minutes, uncover the bowl, fluff the couscous with a fork and set aside.

Meanwhile, heat 3 tablespoons of olive oil in a large saucepan set over medium-low heat. Add the onions, garlic, red chili, thyme, carrots, and a large pinch of salt and cook, stirring now and then, until the vegetables just begin to soften, about 10 minutes. Add the Swiss chard stems, leaves, and another large pinch of salt and cook until the greens are just wilted, about 4 minutes. Lastly, stir in the dates and ¼ cup of water and take the pot off of the heat.

Stir the vegetable mixture into the couscous and allow the mixture to cool.

Lay the lamb on your work surface, cut side up. Place the cooled couscous mixture on the lamb. Roll the lamb like a yoga mat, being careful to keep as much of the couscous mixture inside as possible. Using a few pieces of kitchen string, tie the lamb every couple of inches so it holds together.

Rub the surface of a large roasting pan with olive oil and carefully transfer the lamb to it. Roast the lamb, turning it occasionally, until an instant read thermometer registers 125°F, about 1½ hours depending on the size of the lamb.

Place the honey and the remaining tablespoon of cumin in a small saucepan set over high and heat until the honey is warm and loose, about 1 minute. Pour the warm honey over the lamb and continue to cook, turning the lamb and basting with the excess honey, until the lamb's internal temperature rises to 145°F and the outside is sticky and brown, a final 20 minutes.

Transfer the lamb to a cutting board and let it rest for at least 20 minutes before cutting off and discarding the strings, slicing, and serving.

GREENS, GARLIC + GRAINS

This is all about the heavy dose of garlic. So delicious, simple, healthy, and fast, it's also a very flexible recipe—whatever is green can go in. Serve hot or cold, for breakfast with eggs, as a side dish alongside fish or meat as we've done here, or as the main event itself after a nice soup or salad.

Serves 10

2 cups quinoa, thoroughly rinsed and drained
Coarse salt
5 tablespoons olive oil, divided
12 garlic cloves, peeled and roughly chopped
6 scallions, roughly chopped
2 leeks, white and light green parts only, thinly sliced
2 bunches leafy greens, roughly chopped (such as kale, Swiss chard, or
 spinach)
2 zucchini, ends discarded, thinly sliced into coins
1 small bunch of asparagus, tough ends discarded, cut into 1-inch pieces
A spoonful of Bragg's liquid amino acids* or soy sauce
½ lemon
Freshly ground black pepper

Place the quinoa in a small saucepan and cover with 3½ cups cold water and a large pinch of salt. Bring to a boil over high heat. Lower the heat, cover the pot, and simmer until cooked through, about 12 minutes. Turn off the heat and set the quinoa aside.

Place 3 tablespoons of olive oil in the largest pot you have, preferably a wok, and heat it over medium heat. Add the garlic to the pan and cook, stirring now and then, until softened, 1 minute. Add the scallions, leeks and greens and stir, being sure to get the garlicky olive oil all over everything. After about 2 minutes, once the greens have wilted slightly, stir in the zucchini and asparagus. Cover the pot and allow the vegetables to cook, stirring now and then, until they're all just tender, about 10–15 minutes. Season to taste with salt. Stir in the Bragg's and the quinoa. Transfer to a serving dish and squeeze the juice from the lemon half over the mixture. Drizzle over the remaining 2 tablespoons of olive oil and top it all with a few grinds of black pepper. Serve immediately, at room temperature or cold.

*Bragg's is a liquid protein concentrate that's made from soybeans. It's very similar in appearance and flavor to soy sauce.

RHUBARB ETON MESS

Eton Mess is a traditional British dessert that's wonderfully lazy. Anyone can do it and everyone loves it. You don't have to be good at making pastries or baking. Your meringues can be overcooked or misshapen, but no matter—whipped cream and fruit will make up for everything.

Serves 10

3 large egg whites, at room temperature
¼ cup sugar
Pinch coarse salt
Pinch cream of tartar
Just the rhubarb from 1 batch of Stewed Rhubarb (see page 17)
2 cups heavy cream, whipped
Torn mint leaves for serving

Preheat oven to 200°F.

Line a baking sheet with parchment paper. Combine the eggs whites and sugar in a mixing bowl set over a pot of simmering water, being sure the water doesn't touch the bowl. Stir until the sugar completely dissolves into the egg whites and then remove the bowl from the pot. Stir in the salt and cream of tartar. Place the mixture in the bowl of a stand mixer (or use a hand mixer) and beat until glossy, stiff peaks form, about 5 minutes.

Dollop large spoonfuls of the meringue onto the prepared sheet pan, spacing them evenly apart. Bake until the meringues are crisp to the touch, about 1 hour. Turn off the oven and let the meringues cool completely inside of it, at least another hour.

Break the meringues into pieces and fold them into the whipped cream along with half of the rhubarb. To serve, layer the meringue mixture and the remaining rhubarb in serving dishes or glasses. Garnish with the mint and serve immediately.

SUMMER

AVOCADO TOAST + SPICY SIX-MINUTE EGGS

Avocado toast seems to be everywhere and for good reason—it's so simple, so delicious, so awesome. In our version, we add Six-Minute Eggs because they pretty much improve anything you throw them on.

Serves 4

4 large slices country bread, toasted
¼ cup olive oil
2 avocados, peeled, and pitted and diced
Coarse salt
1 tablespoon white wine vinegar
4 eggs
Large pinch red chili flakes
Your favorite hot sauce (we like Sriracha)
¼ cup cilantro leaves

Drizzle each piece of toast with a tablespoon of olive oil. Evenly distribute the avocado on each piece of toast and use a fork to mash it into the toast. Season each toast with plenty of salt.

To make Six-Minute Eggs, bring a quart of water to a boil and add the vinegar. Carefully place the eggs in the water and boil for exactly 6 minutes. Transfer the eggs to an ice bath for just a minute to stop them from cooking and so that they are cool enough to handle. Peel the eggs and break them in half.

Place the eggs on top of the avocado toast, sprinkle everything with a hefty pinch of red chili flakes and drizzle with plenty of hot sauce. Scatter over the cilantro leaves and serve immediately.

breakfast

ENGLISH BREAKFAST SCRAMBLE

The summer before we opened The Fat Radish, we set up an omelet stand named Two Good Traders at the Hester Street Fair on the Lower East Side in an effort to introduce ourselves to the neighborhood. We had four options: All Greens, Mushroom Madness, Curried Cauliflower, and The Full Monty, which was based on the classic English breakfast. Turned into a scramble, it's an easy and great way to serve a hungry group in the morning.

Serves 4

½ pound chipolata or other breakfast sausages, sliced on the diagonal
    into ½-inch slices
¼ pound sliced bacon, cut into bite-sized pieces
1 cup cherry tomatoes
½ bunch Swiss chard, roughly chopped
8 eggs, whisked together
Small handful chopped chives
Coarse salt and freshly ground black pepper
Buttered toast for serving

Set a large skillet over medium-high heat and place the sausages and bacon in the pan. Cook the meats, stirring now and then, until they're nicely browned and just barely crisp, about 10 minutes. Drain off and discard nearly all of the fat and add the tomatoes to the pan. Cook until the tomatoes just begin to brown and burst in spots, another few minutes. Add the chard to the pan and cook until it's barely wilted, just another couple of minutes. Lastly, add the eggs to the pan and cook, stirring, until they just begin to set. Stir in the chives and season to taste with salt and pepper. Serve immediately with plenty of buttered toast.

SUMMER COCONUT + BERRIES

In this day and age, everyone seems to be gluten- or dairy-free at one point or another and this satisfying, clever sauce is totally vegan and free not just of gluten, but sugar, too. If it's really hot outside, freeze the berries before serving this light and healthy breakfast to make it extra refreshing.

Serves 4

¼ cup cornstarch
1 fresh young coconut, cracked open (or 1½ cups coconut water)
2 cups mixed, ripe summer berries (wild strawberries, blackberries,
    tiny blueberries, etc.)
Small handful torn mint leaves

In a small bowl, stir together the cornstarch and ¼ cup water and set the mixture aside.

Place the liquid from inside the coconut (or the coconut water) into a small pot set over high heat and bring the mixture to a boil. Turn the heat to low and slowly whisk in the cornstarch mixture and allow it to simmer until thickened, about a minute. Transfer the mixture to a blender and blend for a full minute until it's incredibly smooth and a bit of air gets incorporated into it. Set the mixture aside.

Place the berries on a serving platter. Using a small spoon, scrape the meat from the interior of the coconut and scatter it over the berries. (If using coconut water, you can substitute unsweetened coconut flakes). Place dollops of the coconut mixture on top of the berries and scatter with the mint leaves. Serve immediately.

SCOTCH EGGS

Scotch eggs are a traditional British thing, and they are often served at picnics. While they remind us of happy times, in truth, the ones from our youth were never awesome—they were almost always dry, overcooked, and cold. Done right, though, they are a remarkable mix of flavorful sausage meat, eggs with runny yolks, and wonderfully crisp breadcrumbs.

Makes 6

2 tablespoons olive oil
½ medium yellow onion, finely diced
¼ teaspoon ground cloves
¼ teaspoon ground nutmeg
1 tablespoon chopped fresh sage
1 pound fresh pork sausage, casings discarded
Coarse salt and freshly ground black pepper
1 cup flour
2 eggs
2 cups fine breadcrumbs
½ dozen Six-Minute Eggs (see page 68), peeled
Canola oil, for frying
Grainy mustard and cornichons for serving

Place the olive oil in a large, heavy skillet set over medium heat and add the onions. Cook, stirring now and then, until softened but not browned, about 8 minutes. Add the cloves, nutmeg, and sage and cook just until very fragrant, 1 minute. Transfer the mixture to a large bowl and let it cool to room temperature. Once cool, add the sausage, a large pinch each of salt and pepper, and mix well.

Cook a small amount of the sausage mixture in the pan you cooked your onions in to test the mixture for seasoning. Add more spices, salt, and/or pepper if needed.

Place the flour on a large plate. Beat the 2 eggs in a shallow bowl and set that next to the flour plate. Lastly, place the breadcrumbs on a large plate, stir in 2 teaspoons each of salt and pepper, and put the seasoned breadcrumbs next to the bowl of beaten egg.

On a clean, flat work surface, lay out a sheet of plastic wrap about a foot long. Put ⅙ of the sausage meat mixture in the center of the plastic. Pat it down until it forms a small disc that's about ¼-inch thick. Place one of the peeled Six-Minute Eggs in the center of the meat and, using the plastic to help you, pull the meat up around the sides of the egg to totally enclose it. Use your hands on the outside of the plastic to mold the meat around the egg in a neat ball. Transfer the Scotch egg to the plate of flour and roll it to coat. Tap it lightly to remove any excess flour and then dip it into the beaten egg. Next, roll it in breadcrumbs. Place the Scotch egg on a plate and continue the process until you have coated all of the eggs.

Place an inch of canola oil in a large, heavy pot set over medium-high heat. When a small pinch of breadcrumbs bubbles vigorously when placed in the oil, gently place the Scotch eggs into the pot. Fry, turning every so often, until browned all over, about 6–7 minutes all together. Transfer the Scotch eggs to a paper-towel lined plate to cool for a moment and then cut each one in half, sprinkle with a bit of black pepper and serve immediately with mustard and cornichons.

BLUEFISH PATÉ

Bluefish, with its rich, intense flavor, is one of those types of fish that no one eats except for the people who grew up with it. We love it and started serving this paté over the summer to celebrate local bluefish from Long Island. Combining it with cream cheese mellows its flavor and makes it a great dip for vegetables or a spread for toasted grainy bread or bagels.

Makes 2 cups

2 tablespoons butter
1 shallot, minced
2 tablespoons sherry
½ pound smoked bluefish, bones and skin discarded
½ pound cream cheese, at room temperature
2 tablespoons freshly squeezed lemon juice
Coarse salt and freshly ground black pepper

Melt the butter in a small saucepan set over medium heat. Add the shallots and cook, stirring now and then, until softened, about 5 minutes. Add the sherry, turn the heat to high and boil until the sherry is nearly evaporated, about 2 minutes. Set the mixture aside to cool.

Using your hands, break the fish into small pieces. Place the fish into the bowl of a food processor along with the cooled shallot mixture, cream cheese, and lemon juice. Puree until smooth. Season to taste with salt (it might not need any depending on how salty the fish is) and plenty of black pepper.

HEIRLOOM TOMATO + GRILLED SQUASH SALAD WITH KAFFIR LIME DRESSING

We wanted to do an heirloom tomato salad that wasn't just olive oil, salt, and balsamic vinegar (not that there's anything wrong with that). Kaffir lime leaves have such a distinctive, amazing flavor that goes surprisingly well with tomatoes. Use the dressing on just about anything—grilled chicken or shrimp, cooked crab meat, steamed green beans, grilled asparagus, etc. If you can't be bothered to grill the squash, leave it out and just serve the dressing over the tomatoes.

Serves 8

1 garlic clove, roughly chopped
4 scallions, roughly chopped
½ jalapeño (more or less, depending on your taste)
2 fresh kaffir lime leaves (or the zest and juice of 1 lime), finely sliced
    (available at kaffirlimeleaves.com)
1 tablespoon finely chopped fresh ginger
¼ cup rice wine vinegar
1 egg yolk
¾ cup canola oil
Coarse salt
2 pounds summer squash (we love avocado squash, but yellow squash or
    zucchini work well, too), cut into wedges
¼ cup olive oil
2½ pounds mixed heirloom tomatoes, trimmed and stemmed as necessary,
    and halved or cut into wedges depending on their size
A handful of soft herbs (a mix of cilantro leaves, mint, and chives is nice)

Place the garlic, scallions, jalapeño, lime leaves (or lime zest and juice), ginger, and rice wine vinegar in a blender and puree until smooth. Crack in the egg, and blend until smooth. With the blender running, slowly drizzle in the oil until the dressing is emulsified and creamy. Season the dressing to taste with salt.

Meanwhile, preheat grill or grill pan so it's super hot. Use your hands to coat the squash wedges with the olive oil and season aggressively with salt. Grill them, turning now and then, until softened and just slightly charred all over, about 5 minutes. Remove them from the grill and set aside to cool.

Place the grilled squash and the tomatoes on a serving platter and drizzle with the dressing and scatter with the herbs. Serve immediately.

GINGER QUINOA + NORI ROLLS

Sushi can seem daunting, but learning to make it is really fun. Once you've got the technique, the sky's your limit. It makes for a really fun party game, too. You can prepare all of the components and then get your friends about and have everyone do their own rolls. Substituting quinoa for rice makes these extra healthy and protein-packed.

Makes 8 rolls

1 cup quinoa, rinsed and drained
1 (1-inch) knob of ginger, peeled and minced
1 teaspoon coarse salt
8 sheets toasted nori
1 small cucumber, cut into thin strips
1 carrot, peeled and cut into thin strips
1 not-too-ripe avocado, thinly sliced
Small handful sprouts
Soy sauce, for serving

Place the quinoa, ginger, and salt in a small saucepot with 1½ cups of cold water. Bring to a boil. Lower the heat to a simmer, cover the pot, and cook until the quinoa is tender, about 12 minutes. Set the quinoa aside to cool.

Forming one roll at a time, lay a sheet of nori on a dry work surface and place ⅛ of the quinoa on it. Spread the quinoa so it covers half the surface of the nori. Place a vertical strip of the vegetables and sprouts on the quinoa. Dampen your fingers with cold water and spread it on the exposed bit of nori. Tightly roll the roll and slice it into 1-inch pieces. Repeat the process until you've used up all of your nori, quinoa, and vegetables. Serve the rolls with soy sauce.

ONION, TOMATO + CURRY ON TOAST

This is our chef Nick's inventive take on a classic tomato bruschetta. It's one of our favorite dishes at our newest restaurant, The East Pole, on Manhattan's Upper East Side.

Serves 8

Olive oil
2 large yellow onions, thinly sliced
2 pints cherry tomatoes
Coarse salt
8 thick slices toasted country bread
½ cup Curry Sauce (see 86)
Small handful torn basil and cilantro leaves

Preheat oven to 425°F.

Place 3 tablespoons of olive oil in a large, heavy skillet set over medium-low heat. Add the onions and cook, stirring now and then, until well caramelized, 30 minutes. Set the onions aside.

Meanwhile, place the tomatoes in a roasting dish and coat them with 2 tablespoons of olive oil. Roast, stirring now and then, until soft, about 15 minutes. Set the tomatoes aside.

To serve, divide the warm onions and tomatoes over the toast. Drizzle each toast with a tablespoon of the Curry Sauce and top each one with herbs. Serve immediately.

CURRY SAUCE

This makes more than you'll need for Onion, Tomato + Curry on Toast, but it's so delicious that you might as well make the whole batch. Use the rest to cook vegetables in for a quick, healthy dinner or use it to dress cooked chicken, fish, or shrimp. Stretched out with vegetable or chicken stock, this also makes a lovely soup.

Makes 2½ cups

2 tablespoons coconut oil or olive oil
2 garlic cloves, thinly sliced
1 yellow onion, thinly sliced
1 green apple, peeled and cored, thinly sliced
1 (2-inch) knob of ginger, peeled and minced
1 kaffir lime leaf* (available at kaffirlimeleaves.com)
1½ tablespoons curry powder
2 teaspoons turmeric
1 (13.5-ounce) can unsweetened coconut milk
Coarse salt

Place the oil in a saucepan set over medium heat. Add the garlic, onion, fennel, apple, ginger, lime leaf, curry powder, and turmeric and cook, stirring now and then, until softened, about 10 minutes. Add the coconut milk, bring the sauce to a boil, lower the heat to a simmer and cook until the vegetables are tender, about 10 minutes. Remove and discard the lime leaf and puree the sauce with an immersion blender or in a standard blender. Season to taste with salt.

*If you can't find kaffir lime, stir in the zest and juice from a lime once the sauce is blended.

Summer adventures on the road with The Radish

This page, clockwise from top left: Phil and the team take a break from cooking at a music festival on Long Island. The ultimate mobile grill. Tarragon and mint mojitos, the best drink for summer cookouts. Ben heads to the beach to cook the fish he caught that day—we think he momentarily forgot that he was British when it came to sunscreen. **Opposite page, from left:** Easiest and best thing on the grill: whole corn with chili butter and lime. On the way to surf in Montauk—the best thing about running a restaurant by the ocean. The mobile Fat Radish at the Escape to New York festival.

GRILLED SUMMER SQUASH WITH KALE PESTO

Kale seems ubiquitous these days, but when we did a pop-up restaurant in Paris, it was almost impossible to find. We managed to track some down and made loads of this kale pesto, and we like to think we brought the kale craze to Paris... Note that this pesto is equally good on pasta or served alongside grilled fish.

Serves 4

Coarse salt
½ bunch kale, roughly chopped
6 cloves roasted garlic (see page 132)
¼ cup pine nuts, lightly toasted
¼ cup grated pecorino cheese, plus extra for serving
Zest and juice of ½ a lemon
¼ cup extra virgin olive oil, plus more for grilling
2 pounds summer squash (we love avocado squash, but yellow squash or
   zucchini work well, too), cut into wedges

Bring a large pot of water to a boil and liberally salt it. Place the kale in the boiling water and cook until it's bright green and just-tender, about 5 minutes. Drain the kale, rinse it with cool water, and use your hands to squeeze out all of the liquid.

Place the kale into the bowl of a food processor along with the roasted garlic, pine nuts, pecorino, lemon zest, and lemon juice. Pulse until everything is very finely chopped and then, with the machine running, slowly drizzle in the olive oil. Season the pesto to taste with salt and set aside.

Meanwhile, preheat grill or grill pan so it's super hot. Use your hands to coat the squash wedges with a few tablespoons of olive oil and season aggressively with salt. Grill them, turning now and then, until softened and just slightly charred all over, about 5 minutes. Transfer the squash to a serving platter, spoon over the pesto, and serve immediately.

SWEET CORN + CHERRY TOMATO SUCCOTASH WITH CRAB

Summers working in Montauk exposed us to Long Island's sweet corn, which seems to explode out of the ground. We love combining the corn with crab, but feel free to leave it out if you're vegetarian (or if crab's a bit too pricy)—this succotash is equally good without it.

Serves 4

4 ears corn, shucked
1 small zucchini, cut lengthwise into ¼-inch thick slices
Olive oil
½ cup crème fraîche
1 cup cherry tomatoes, halved
Small handful fresh dill, roughly chopped
½ pound cleaned crab meat
Coarse salt and freshly ground black pepper

Preheat grill or grill pan so it's super hot. Use your hands to coat the corn and zucchini all over with a little bit of oil. Grill the vegetables, turning them now and then, until slightly charred all over, about 5 minutes. Remove them from the grill and set aside to cool.

Once cool enough to handle, dice the zucchini and place it in a large bowl. Cut the kernels off the cobs, discarding the cobs. Place half the corn kernels in the bowl with the zucchini and place the other half in a blender with the crème fraîche. Blend until completely smooth and add the puree to the bowl along with the tomatoes, dill, and crab meat. Season the succotash to taste with salt and pepper. Serve immediately.

NICK'S MOM'S CUCUMBER SALAD WITH FRIED OYSTERS

Nick's favorite dish in the whole world is his mother Mary-Ellen's cucumber salad. He even served it at his wedding and sent everyone home with a recipe card. Nick brought this dish to The Fat Radish where it's had many different lives. This version, with crunchy fried oysters, is the latest, and quite possibly the best, incarnation.

Serves 4

1½ English cucumbers, ends trimmed off and discarded, thinly sliced
¼ cup Champagne or white wine vinegar
Coarse salt
¼ cup fresh dill, roughly chopped
½ red onion, very thinly sliced
½ cup puffed rice cereal
2 tablespoons toasted sesame seeds
2 tablespoons nori seaweed flakes
1 dozen shucked oysters
Peanut oil for frying (or whatever oil you like for frying)
3 tablespoons crème fraîche or sour cream

In a large bowl, stir together the cucumbers, vinegar, a pinch of salt, 3 tablespoons of the dill, and the onion. Let the salad sit while you prepare the oysters.

Place the cereal, sesame seeds, and seaweed flakes in a food processor and pulse until the mixture is finely ground (but not dust). Transfer the mixture to a bowl. Dredge the oysters in the mixture, shaking off any excess and discarding whatever you don't use.

Heat an inch of oil in a large, heavy pot over medium-high heat. Carefully place the oysters in the oil and fry, turning once, until crisp, about 3 minutes all together. Be very cautious while frying oysters as they tend to splatter. Use a slotted spoon to transfer the oysters to a paper towel-lined plate and sprinkle each one with a tiny pinch of salt.

Use a slotted spoon to transfer the cucumber salad to a large platter, reserving the leftover liquid. Place the oysters on the salad. Whisk the crème fraîchè or sour cream into whatever liquid is left in the bowl and drizzle over the entire thing. Garnish with the remaining tablespoon of dill and serve immediately.

WATERMELON + CUCUMBER SALAD WITH CHILI + CHARRED SHALLOT DRESSING

The dressing comes from Matty B., a great chef who used to cook for us. An English guy who had cooked Thai food in Australia, Matty B. introduced us to this dressing, which we adore for its balanced combination of spicy, sweet, sour, and salty (the four distinctive traits of Thai cooking).

Serves 4

1 tablespoon olive oil
4 dried arbol chilies, stems and seeds discarded
2 shallots (unpeeled)
¼ cup turbinado (raw) sugar
¼ cup freshly squeezed lime juice
2 tablespoons fish sauce
1½ pounds (4 cups) roughly diced watermelon, seeds discarded
1 large English cucumber, roughly diced
Small handful cilantro leaves, roughly chopped

Place the olive oil in a heavy skillet set over high heat and add the chilies to the pan. Cook, stirring now and then, until fragrant, just a minute. Transfer the chilies to a mortar and pestle and place the shallots into the same skillet. Cook the shallots until charred all over, a few minutes, and then add ¼ cup of water, turn the heat to low and cover the pan. Cook the shallots until soft, about 5 minutes. Turn off the heat and allow the shallots to cool to room temperature. Once cool, peel the shallots and discard the skins. Set the shallots aside.

Pound the chilies together with the sugar in the mortar and pestle (alternatively, you can do this in a food processor) until the sugar turns red. Add the reserved shallots to the mixture and pound to form a smooth paste. Add the lime juice and fish sauce and stir to combine. Season to taste with more sugar, lime juice, and/or fish sauce.

Combine the watermelon and cucumber in a bowl and coat with the dressing. Serve immediately, with cilantro leaves scattered on top.

Dream come true, cooking the Outstanding in the Field dinner.

This page, from left: Guests at the 2013 Outstanding in the Field dinner at Brooklyn Grange Farm, with the New York skyline in the background. Phil puts the finishing touches on his smoked tomato and sausage pasta. Phil Lewis, our chef de cuisine, prepares the evening's canapés.
Opposite page, clockwise from top left: Simple, elegant table settings, and a menu created with ingredients grown on the rooftop farm. Family style is the best way to serve large groups—and so much fun at the table. Two guests enjoy the magical Outstanding evening. Jim Denevan, chef, artist and founder of Outstanding in the Field, chats with Nick about the menu.

PEACHES WITH PROSCIUTTO + MASCARPONE

We basically owe everything to this incredibly simple hors d'oeuvre. We served it all the time when we were caterers and it was just the sort of unpretentious, approachable bite that people loved and remembered us for.

Makes 16 hors d'oeuvres

2 ripe peaches, halved and pitted
16 small basil leaves
¼ pound thinly sliced prosciutto
½ cup mascarpone cheese
1 tablespoon balsamic vinegar

Slice each peach half into four wedges. Place a piece of basil on each wedge and wrap each one with a slice of prosciutto. Spread the mascarpone artfully on a serving platter and use it to anchor the peaches. Drizzle the balsamic vinegar over the peaches. Serve immediately, encouraging guests to swipe their peaches through the mascarpone.

FAT RADISH CHEESEBURGER

Until you've lived in the States, you have no idea what hamburger culture is or how important it is. Like football (soccer) in England, everyone has an informed opinion about burgers and allegiances are loyal and fierce. Our cheeseburger is incredibly simple and relies on plenty of beef fat for flavor and juiciness. Served with our Homemade Pickles and Duck Fat Fries, it's our humble attempt to fit in.

Makes 4 burgers

1¾ pounds ground beef (ask your butcher to do a grind of 70% chuck
    and 30% shortrib)
Coarse salt and freshly ground black pepper
4 thick slices clothbound cheddar cheese
4 brioche hamburger buns, halved and toasted
4 large leaves of butter lettuce
A dozen slices cooked bacon (optional)
1 very ripe tomato, sliced

Preheat grill or grill pan so the heat is medium-hot. Using your hands, gently shape the beef into 4 burgers. Season each burger aggressively with salt and pepper on both sides. Grill the burgers until they're cooked to your liking and then top each one with a thick slice of cheddar. Close your grill or cover your grill pan with an inverted stainless steel bowl so that the cheese melts. Once the cheese is melted, transfer the burgers to the toasted buns and dress with lettuce, tomato, and bacon. Serve immediately.

HOMEMADE PICKLES

The Lower East Side is home not just to The Fat Radish, but also to the pickle. Historically, there were many pickle vendors were in our neighborhood and luckily there are still a few left. Our recipe is based on their perfect, traditional, New York-style pickles.

Makes 1 pound

1 pound Kirby cucumbers, cut in half lengthwise or cut into coins, whatever
   you prefer
1 white onion, thinly sliced
2 garlic cloves, thinly sliced
2 tablespoons coarse salt
3 cups white wine vinegar
⅔ cup sugar
1 teaspoon turmeric
1 teaspoon mustard seeds

Place the cucumbers, onion, and garlic in a large bowl and sprinkle with the salt. Use your hands to toss everything together. Place a slightly smaller bowl or plate on top and put a few tins of tomatoes or beans or something else heavy on top to weigh the vegetables down. Let the cucumbers sit for half an hour, drain them, and set them aside.

Meanwhile, combine the vinegar, sugar, turmeric, and mustard seeds in a saucepan set over medium-high heat. Bring the mixture to a boil, stir to dissolve the sugar and then pour the hot mixture over the drained cucumbers. Once everything cools down, pack everything into a jar or a container, cover, and refrigerate for at least 24 hours before eating. These last in the fridge up to a month.

DUCK FAT FRIES

In the UK, duck fat is hugely popular for roasting potatoes in. What's great about these fries is, up to the point of browning them off in the pan, they can be made ahead of time. To make these extra special, spike mayonnaise with a few drops of truffle oil and serve it alongside the fries for dipping.

Serves 4

2 russet potatoes, cut into thick wedges
1 quart (4 cups) duck fat, melted
1 head of garlic, halved across the middle
Small handful fresh thyme
Coarse salt and freshly ground black pepper
Finely chopped chives and finely grated Parmesan for serving

Preheat oven to 325°F.

Rinse the potatoes and pat them dry. Place them in a baking dish that fits them snugly and pour the duck fat over. Tuck in the garlic and thyme, cover, and place the dish in the oven. Bake until the potatoes are tender (test with the tip of a paring knife), about 45 minutes. Remove and discard the garlic and thyme and transfer the potatoes to paper towels to drain.

When you're ready to serve, heat 2 tablespoons of the duck fat in a large nonstick skillet set over medium-high heat and add an even layer of potatoes. Cook the potatoes, turning once, until browned on both sides, about 2 minutes a side. Transfer the potatoes to a serving platter. Repeat the process, using more duck fat as needed, until all of the potatoes are browned.

Season the potatoes with salt and pepper and scatter with the chives and Parmesan. Serve immediately.

*Leftover duck fat should not be discarded! Use it for roasting potatoes or fish, or use it like butter on grilled bread and top with roasted garlic and cooked greens (see page 132), or for Duck Confit Terrine (see page 197).

GRILLED STEAK WITH ROASTED GARLIC + ARUGULA CHIMICHURRI

This simple, untraditional chimichurri highlights the earthy, rich flavor of really good red meat. Choose whatever steak suits your budget and cook it lovingly—the cut doesn't matter, only the quality. While your grill is on, throw on a few ears of corn and add a bowl of Sautéed Greens (page 213) or any other vegetable to turn this into a complete meal.

Serves 4

8 cloves roasted garlic (see page 132), smashed to a paste
1 small shallot, minced
1 large handful arugula, finely chopped
1 tablespoon red wine vinegar
Olive oil
Coarse salt
Freshly ground black pepper
1½ pounds steak (we like hanger, skirt, and ribeye best on the grill)

In a small bowl, stir together the garlic paste, shallot, arugula, vinegar, ½ cup of olive oil, and ½ teaspoon each salt and pepper. Set the chimichurri aside.

Meanwhile, preheat your grill or grill pan so the heat is super hot. Rub the steak with a bit of olive oil and season aggressively with salt and pepper. Grill to your liking and then remove the steak to a board and let it rest for at least 10 minutes. Slice the steak against the grain and serve immediately with the chimichurri.

"All work and No play can make life very dull"

This page, clockwise from top left: Catch of the day, a beautiful striped bass. Ben gets the fire ready for cooking at the beach. An old friend makes sure Ben and Phil don't drown in the surf. Phil heads out for day of fishing in Montauk. Opposite page, clockwise from left: Striped Bass with roasted peppers and charred corn. Fishing is not Ben's strength, but he might have better luck if he looked at the pole. Time to eat.

GRILLED WHOLE FISH WITH SPICY RED GRAPE SALSA

Nothing could be both as easy and impressive as a whole grilled fish. Use whatever type of fish that swims near you and feel free to improvise with various aromatics and herbs—this is a real throw-in-anything kind of recipe. The spicy red grape salsa makes this fish especially memorable.

Serves 4

2 cups seedless red grapes, washed and quartered
1 jalapeño, seeded and finely diced
2 tablespoons finely diced red onion
¼ cup roughly chopped fresh cilantro
Zest and juice of 1 lime
Olive oil
2 (1½-pound each) whole snapper or branzino, gutted and scaled
Coarse salt and freshly ground black pepper
1 small fennel bulb, thinly sliced
A handful of leafy herbs

Place the grapes, jalapeño, red onion, cilantro, lime zest and juice, and 2 tablespoons of olive oil in a bowl and stir together. Set the salsa aside.

Score each fish a few times on each side being careful not to cut too deeply. Season the skin and cavity of each fish generously with salt and pepper. Stuff each fish with half of the fennel and herbs and rub the outside of each fish with a tablespoon of oil.

Prepare a medium-hot fire in a charcoal grill, or heat a gas grill to medium. Alternatively, heat a grill pan on your stove set over medium heat.

Grill each fish until the skin no longer sticks, about 5 minutes on the first side. Using a metal spatula, carefully turn each fish and grill until the second side no longer sticks and the flesh is firm to the touch, about 3–4 more minutes. Transfer the fish to a platter and serve immediately with the spicy red grape salsa.

FREGOLA WITH CHARRED PEPPERS, PINE NUTS + LEMON DRESSING

This is a really flexible recipe. You can put pretty much any vegetable or grain you want in here as long as there are loads of herbs and plenty of bright lemon. We love nutty Sardinian fregola—a small, toasted pasta—here, but truly any grain works!

Serves 4

2 cups vegetable stock
1 cup fregola sarda (or you can substitute Israeli couscous)
Olive oil
1 red bell pepper, stem and seeds discarded, diced
Handful shishito peppers (or a diced green bell pepper), stemmed and
    roughly chopped
1 cup cherry tomatoes
½ bunch Swiss chard, roughly chopped
¼ cup toasted pine nuts
1 cup roughly chopped leafy herbs (a combination of mostly parsley and
    chives with a little tarragon is our go-to)
Juice of 1 lemon
Coarse salt and freshly ground black pepper

Bring the stock to a boil in a saucepan and stir in the fregola. Cook until the fregola is tender, about 10 minutes. Drain, discarding the excess cooking liquid, and place in a large bowl. Set aside.

Meanwhile, place 2 tablespoons of the olive oil in a large skillet set over high heat. Add the peppers and cook, stirring a bit, until they're a bit charred and softened, just a few minutes. Add the tomatoes and cook until they are slightly charred, too, and some of them begin to split, 1–2 minutes. Lastly, add the chard to the pan and cook until it wilts, about 2 minutes. Transfer the vegetables to the bowl with the fregola and stir in the pine nuts, herbs, and lemon juice. Season to taste with salt and pepper. Serve at room temperature.

ROASTED STONE FRUIT WITH VANILLA + MASCARPONE

All the effort of this dish is in picking the fruit. It's a dessert that is all about capturing what's in season and celebrating fruit at its peak. Anyone who has food as a priority in their life is the person touching, smelling, and evaluating every single piece of fruit they buy. Be that person!

Serves 4

1½ pounds ripe stone fruit (we like a mix of nectarines, peaches, and
   apricots), pits discarded, cut into thick wedges if large or halved if small
1 vanilla bean, halved lengthwise
¼ cup sugar
Pinch of freshly grated nutmeg
Mascarpone for serving

Preheat oven to 425°F.

Place the fruit in a large baking dish that fits it comfortably in a relatively even layer. Tuck in the vanilla bean and sprinkle with the sugar and the nutmeg. Use your hands to combine all of the ingredients and pop the dish into the oven. Roast the fruit, stirring now and then, until it's softened and releases tons of juice, about 20 minutes. Serve warm with spoonfuls of mascarpone.

FALL

BROWN RICE OATMEAL

Brown rice is something we always seem to cook in abundance. This super simple, healthy breakfast is the best use of leftover rice we know. If you don't have leftover cooked rice, simply cook a cup of rice according to package directions and then follow the recipe as described (a cup of raw rice will yield 2 cups of cooked rice).

Serves 4

2 cups milk
1 (2-inch) knob of ginger, peeled and thinly sliced
2 cups leftover cooked brown rice
Maple syrup or honey, for serving
Almonds and sunflower seeds (or whatever nuts you'd like), for serving
Raspberries and blueberries (or whatever fruit you'd like), for serving

Place the milk and ginger in a saucepan set over medium heat. Once bubbles form around the edge, turn the heat down, add the rice, and cook, stirring a bit, until the rice is warm and has absorbed most of the milk, about 10 minutes. Serve hot, topped with maple syrup or honey, nuts and berries, or whatever combination of the aforementioned suits your taste.

MUSHROOMS ON TOAST WITH FRIED EGGS

We get our eggs and mushrooms from a farmer named Ben Shaw who is based in the Adirondacks, a few hours upstate from New York City. He has 13 children and each has his or her own specialty on the farm. One of his sons grows mushrooms in their barn (hence his nickname, "Fun Guy"). This combination of the two ingredients makes for a memorable brunch dish.

Serves 4

4 cups baby arugula
1 tablespoon sherry vinegar
Olive oil
1 pound mixed wild mushrooms, roughly chopped
2 sprigs of thyme
1 head garlic, cut in half across the middle
Coarse salt
Freshly ground black pepper
3 tablespoons butter
4 eggs
4 thick slices of buttered whole grain toast
Shaved pecorino cheese for serving

Place the arugula in a large bowl and evenly drizzle the vinegar over the leaves. Set aside.

Meanwhile, place 3 tablespoons of the olive oil in a large skillet, preferably nonstick, set over high heat. Add the mushrooms, thyme, and garlic and cook, stirring now and then, until the mushrooms just begin to soften and brown, about 5 minutes. Season the mushrooms with salt and pepper and add the butter. Turn the heat to medium and, once the butter begins to turn a little bit brown, about 2 minutes, remove the pan from the heat. Discard the thyme and garlic. Pour the mushroom mixture over the arugula and toss to combine (the arugula will wilt a little—that's okay).

Place the pan back over the heat and add 2 more tablespoons of olive oil. Crack the eggs into the pan and cover the pan. Cook the eggs until the whites are just set, about 3 minutes.

Place a slice of toast on each of 4 dishes. Evenly distribute the arugula and mushrooms over the toast. Place a fried egg on top of each portion and scatter with a bit of shaved pecorino. Serve immediately.

CINNAMON + SUGAR HOLE-LESS DONUTS

You're never going to have a better donut than one you make yourself. Only at home can you enjoy them the moment they're done, while they're still hot. Even though the dough has to rest overnight, these are really quite simple and worth the time it takes to make them.

Makes 2 dozen

3 cups all-purpose flour, plus extra for rising and shaping
¼ cup sugar
1 teaspoon salt
1 sachet dry active yeast
2 large eggs, beaten
Zest of 1 lemon
½ cup water
1 stick (8 tablespoons) cold butter, diced
Vegetable oil for frying
Cinnamon sugar for rolling

Place the flour, sugar, salt, yeast, eggs, lemon zest, and water in a stand mixer fitted with a paddle attachment (or in a bowl with a handheld mixer). Set the mixer to medium and let everything come together into a thick batter, just a minute. Add the butter to the mixture and let the mixer run on medium until the dough begins to pull away from the sides of the bowl and becomes incredibly elastic, about 10 minutes of mixing (think of it like your machine doing the kneading for you).

Dust the interior of a large bowl with flour and transfer the dough to it. Dust the surface of the dough with a bit more flour. Cover with plastic wrap and place in the refrigerator overnight.

The following day, remove the dough from the refrigerator and allow it to come to room temperature. Dust a baking sheet with flour and set it aside.

Divide the dough into 24 pieces and roll each into a ball. Place them on the floured tray and drape with a clean kitchen towel. Set the tray in a warm place until the dough balls double in size, about an hour.

Meanwhile, heat 2 inches of oil in a large, heavy pot set over medium-high heat until it reaches 375°F (or until a pinch of flour sizzles on contact). Dust the excess flour from the donuts and carefully place them in the hot oil in batches so that each has plenty of space around it. Fry, turning occasionally, until browned on all sides, about 5 minutes total. Transfer the browned donuts to a paper towel-lined plate or tray to drain. Immediately roll in plenty of cinnamon sugar and serve hot.

Bringing the table to the farm and making a few new friends.

KABOCHA SOUP

This super creamy, rich soup is completely vegan. How about that?!

Serves 6

One 3-pound kabocha squash
Coarse salt
3 tablespoons olive oil
1 onion, finely diced
4 garlic cloves, finely chopped
1 teaspoon ground turmeric
3 cups vegetable stock
1 (15-ounce) can unsweetened coconut milk
¼ cup toasted pumpkin seeds
Small handful chopped chives

Preheat the oven to 425°F.

Cut the kabocha in half and scoop out and discard the seeds and the stringy flesh inside. Wrap the cleaned squash in aluminum foil and place in the oven. Roast until softened, about an hour. Set the squash aside.

Meanwhile, place the olive oil in a large, heavy pot set over medium-high heat. Add the onion, garlic, turmeric, and a pinch of salt and cook, stirring now and then, until beginning to soften, about 10 minutes. Add the stock and coconut milk, bring the mixture to a boil, lower the heat and simmer while you prepare the squash.

Peel off and discard the skin from half of the roasted squash and add the flesh to the soup. Use an immersion blender to puree. Season to taste with salt.

Cut the remaining half of roasted squash into wedges and place them in the soup. Serve the soup hot, garnishing each serving with toasted pumpkin seeds and a sprinkle of chives.

GREENS ON TOAST WITH ROASTED GARLIC BUTTER

This is our version of garlic bread: heavy on the greens. We find that Swiss chard, kale, spinach, and the like are sweetest in fall because once it gets cool out, greens, just like grapes, scrunch down and flex to withstand the drop in temperature, giving up their water and concentrating their sugar in the process.

Makes 1 dozen toasts

1 head garlic, top ¼-inch cut off and discarded (or enough to expose
   the individual garlic cloves)
Olive oil
Zest and juice of 1 lemon
Leaves from 1 small bunch fresh parsley, finely chopped
¼ cup softened butter
Freshly ground black pepper
1 bunch Swiss chard, roughly chopped
1 loaf country bread, thickly sliced and toasted

Preheat the oven to 375°F.

Place the garlic in the center of a piece of aluminum foil and drizzle with 2 teaspoons of olive oil. Wrap the garlic in the foil and place in the oven until the cloves are a little bit browned and completely soft, about half an hour.

Allow the garlic to cool to room temperature before squeezing the cloves out from the skin. Discard the skin.

Place the roasted garlic, lemon zest and juice, parsley, and butter in a large mixing bowl along with ½ a teaspoon each of coarse salt and pepper. Use a fork to mash it all up into a cohesive but not too-smooth mixture. Set the mixture aside.

Place 2 tablespoons of olive oil in a large skillet set over high heat and add the Swiss chard. Cook, stirring now and then, until it's just wilted, a few minutes. Season the chard to taste with salt and pepper and set it aside.

Spread each piece of toast generously with the roasted garlic butter and top each with some of the chard. Serve immediately.

CARROT + AVOCADO SALAD WITH HIJIKI + CRISPY KALE

This salad is a larger version of a canapé we often made when we started off as caterers. We ate so much of this for so many years that we can't even eat it anymore! Luckily, our customers still love it.

Serves 6

¼ cup soy sauce
2 tablespoons sesame oil
¼ cup mirin
2 teaspoons fish sauce
1 garlic clove, minced
1 teaspoon freshly grated ginger
½ ounce dried hijiki (about ¼ cup), rinsed and soaked in warm water for
   15 minutes, drained
1 bunch curly kale, leaves torn into small pieces, stems discarded
5 tablespoons olive oil, divided
½ teaspoon Chinese five spice powder
½ teaspoon coarse salt
2 pounds heirloom carrots, scrubbed, ends trimmed
2 ripe avocados, peeled, pitted, and cut into wedges

In a mixing bowl, whisk together the soy sauce, sesame oil, mirin, fish sauce, garlic, and ginger. Add the drained hijiki and set the mixture aside.

Preheat oven to 325°F.

Place the kale on a baking sheet and drizzle with 2 tablespoons of the olive oil. Sprinkle with five spice powder and salt. Place the kale in the oven and bake, turning the leaves once, until crispy, about 20 minutes. Set the kale aside.

Bring a large pot of salted water to a boil and add the carrots. Cook until they're nearly tender, about 10 minutes. Transfer the carrots to a paper towel-lined plate to drain and cut them in half lengthwise.

Place the remaining 3 tablespoons of olive oil in a large, heavy skillet and set it over medium-high heat. Add the carrots to the pan and cook, stirring until caramelized, about 10 minutes. Transfer the carrots to a large bowl.

Spoon the hijiki and its marinade over the carrots, add the crispy kale and the avocado wedges and stir gently to combine. Serve immediately.

PEACH CEVICHE WITH RAW FLUKE

In New York, peach season extends into fall; in fact, that's when they're best. Here, instead of garnishing a fish ceviche with peaches, we invert the ratio and use the fish as a complement to slightly unripe peaches. Super squishy ripe fruit is delicious and sweet, but this recipe shows how not-quite-ripe fruit can serve a purpose, too. The firmer slices have wonderful texture and great acidity, and work well in a savory preparation like this. As it were, feel free to skip the fluke and serve the peach ceviche on anything, including tortilla chips.

Serves 4

⅓ cup amaretto liqueur
2 hard peaches (not too ripe), pitted and cut into a fine dice
Juice and zest of 2 limes
1 jalapeño, stem and seeds discarded, minced
2 tablespoons finely chopped cilantro
Coarse salt and freshly ground black pepper
½ pound fluke, very thinly sliced
2 tablespoons extra virgin olive oil
Small handful small greens or leafy herbs (such as purslane or chervil)

Place the amaretto in a small saucepan and bring to a boil. Cook until it becomes a thick syrup, about 2–3 minutes. Pour the syrup into a large bowl and add the peaches, lime juice and zest, jalapeño, and cilantro. Season the mixture to taste with salt and pepper.

Arrange the fluke on a large, preferably chilled, serving platter and drizzle with the olive oil. Season with salt and pepper and then cover it with the peach mixture. Scatter with greens and serve immediately.

CHICKPEAS, CHORIZO + TOMATOES WITH BLUEFISH + MUSSELS

This dish straddles summer and fall and is great for when the air just begins to get cool. We like bluefish in this because we first started making this dish out on Long Island, where bluefish populates the local waters. Feel free to use mackerel, or any oily, rich fish. Serve this hearty stew with plenty of rustic bread.

Serves 6

3 tablespoons olive oil
1 link (4 ounces) dried chorizo, thinly sliced
1 large yellow onion, diced
1 cup dried chickpeas, soaked overnight in cold water and drained
3 cups vegetable stock
1 pound tomatoes, cored and chopped
Coarse salt
2 ½ pounds bluefish filets, skin discarded, cut into chunks
1 pound mussels, scrubbed
A large handful of parsley and/or chervil leaves

Place the olive oil in a large, heavy pot set over medium-high heat. Add the chorizo and cook, stirring now and then, until it's crisp and its fat has rendered, about 2 minutes. Use a slotted spoon to transfer the chorizo to a plate and set aside.

Add the onion to the pot and cook, stirring now and then, until softened, about 10 minutes. Add the drained chickpeas to the onions along with the stock and tomatoes. Bring the mixture to a boil, lower the heat, and simmer until the chickpeas are tender, about an hour or two depending on their age (the older the bean, the longer it will take to soften).

Stir the reserved chorizo back into the mix and season to taste with salt. Nestle the fish into the mixture and place the mussels on top of the fish. Cover the pot and cook until the fish is cooked through and the mussels are opened, about 10 minutes. Give the mixture a good stir, sprinkle with herbs, and serve immediately.

HONEY + ORANGE DUCK WITH ROASTED FENNEL

Duck seems so cheffy, but really it's so easy. Try serving this for a dinner party—people will think you really know what you're doing when it hits the table. In fact, we developed this dish to serve when Phil's dad had the ambassador of Japan over for dinner. (Don't ask.) We loved it so much that we put it on the opening menu of The Fat Radish.

Serves 6

3 fennel bulbs, stems and tough outer leaves discarded, sliced, and a
    handful of fronds reserved for garnish
1 cup vegetable stock
½ cup sugar
2 teaspoons coriander seeds, crushed
2 teaspoons fennel seeds, crushed
1 (2-inch) cinnamon stick
2 star anise
2 bay leaves
½ teaspoon dried red chili flakes
1 garlic clove, thinly sliced
1 (1-inch) knob fresh ginger, peeled and finely sliced
Zest and juice of 1 orange, plus another orange cut into half moons
2 tablespoons honey
2 tablespoons soy sauce
2 teaspoons fish sauce
4 large duck breasts, patted dry with paper towels, each cut into 3 pieces

Preheat the oven to 425°F.

Place the fennel and vegetable stock in a large roasting dish and cover with foil. Roast, uncovering the dish and stirring the fennel now and then, until just softened, about 20 minutes. Uncover the fennel and roast until caramelized, another 15 minutes. Set the fennel aside.

Meanwhile, place the sugar in a saucepan with 2 tablespoons of water set over medium-high heat. Cook, stirring until the sugar melts and comes to a boil. Lower the heat and allow the mixture to simmer, swirling the pot now and then by its handle, until it browns and turns into a caramel. Add the spices, garlic, ginger, orange zest and juice, honey, soy sauce, and fish sauce to the pot (be careful, as the caramel will boil vigorously when the additional liquid is introduced). Cook the mixture until the caramel dissolves into the new ingredients and everything boils down to a thick glaze, about 5 minutes. Set the glaze aside.

Place the duck breasts skin side down in a large, ovenproof skillet that fits them without crowding. Set the skillet over medium-low heat and cook the duck breasts until the fat is rendered and the skin is crisp, about 15–20 minutes. Use tongs to transfer the duck breasts to the baking dish with the roasted fennel. Reserve the fat left in the pan for another use. (See Duck Fat Fries on page 105).

Pour the glaze over the duck and scatter over the half moon slices of orange. Place the roasting dish in the oven and roast until the duck is nicely glazed and just firm to the touch, about 10 minutes. Serve immediately, sprinkled with the reserved fennel fronds.

A typical day in the Restaurant

This page, clockwise from top left: The entrance to the restaurant, with our signature swing stools. Cauliflower mash. Ben gets the restaurant ready for service. Opposite page clockwise from top left: Nick writes the day's specials after his morning trip to the market. Roasted fennel. The view of the Manhattan Bridge from the rooftop of the restaurant. Slavica Dragojevic, our wonderful general manager and the greatest florist in New York— she takes the flowers as seriously as we take food.

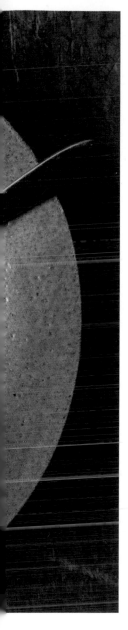

MONKFISH VINDALOO

We've always had a different curry on the menu at our restaurants. (Curry is the official British national dish!) This is the one we had on the menu when we first opened The Fat Radish. The paste comes straight from Rick Stein, a renowned English chef for whom Ben used to work. Vindaloo is usually blow-your-head-off hot, but instead of straight-up heat, this one also has wonderful, warm spices.

Serves 6

Paste
2 yellow onions, unpeeled
4 Kashmiri chilies, soaked overnight in water, drained and chopped (discard stems)*
½ teaspoon ground cloves
1 teaspoon ground cinnamon
2 teaspoons ground cumin
2 teaspoons freshly ground black pepper
1 teaspoon coarse salt
1 (2-inch knob) fresh ginger root, minced
4 garlic cloves, minced
1 tablespoon brown sugar
2 tablespoons tamarind pulp (worth finding, but if you can't, substitute the zest and juice of 2 limes)
¼ cup white wine vinegar

Finished Dish
2 tablespoons olive oil
1 yellow onion, thinly sliced
2 plum tomatoes, cored and finely chopped
1 cup vegetable or fish stock (or water)
2½ pounds monkfish, cut into bite-sized pieces
Cooked rice, yogurt or Tzatziki (see page 53), and fresh herbs for serving

For the vindaloo paste, preheat the oven to 400°F and wrap the onions in a piece of tin foil. Roast until completely soft, about an hour. Let the onions cool and then peel them. Place the roasted onion flesh in a blender or food processor along with the remaining paste ingredients and puree until smooth. Set the paste aside.

For the finished dish, place the oil in a large saucepan set over-medium high heat. Add the sliced onion and cook, stirring now and then, until softened and browned, about 10 minutes. Add the reserved vindaloo paste and cook, stirring now and then, until the entire mixture is quite dry, about 10 minutes. Add the tomatoes and stock, bring the mixture to a boil and then lower the heat to a simmer. Season to taste with salt.

Place the monkfish pieces into the curry, cover the pot, and cook until the monkfish is cooked through, about 10–15 minutes. Serve the monkfish with plenty of rice, yogurt or Tzatziki, and a few herbs on top.

*If you can't find Kashmiri chilies, you can use arbol chilies or substitute 1 tablespoon each ground cayenne and sweet paprika.

SCALLOPS WITH SWEET POTATO + GOLDEN BEET MASH + CAPER SALSA VERDE

We always try to celebrate what's in season and this scallop dish is really all about the autumn-tinged mash underneath it. The sweet and soft combination of sweet potatoes and golden beets is countered with a tart dressing and big, juicy scallops. This is a great dish for a dinner party since the dressing and mash can be made ahead and the impressive-looking scallops take just minutes to prepare. Note that if you can't get scallops or don't like them, any fish will work here.

Serves 6

3 tablespoons capers, roughly chopped
1 tablespoon grainy mustard
2 tablespoons freshly squeezed lemon juice
1 cup finely chopped soft herbs (i.e., mint, cilantro, basil, tarragon, and/or dill)
½ cup olive oil
Coarse salt
1 pound each sweet potatoes and golden beets, peeled and roughly chopped
4 tablespoons butter
A few sprigs thyme
1 dozen very large day boat sea scallops (or 2 dozen regular sea scallops),
    tough muscle discarded, patted dry with paper towels
Crème fraîche for serving
Handful of cooked greens or chopped parsley for serving

Place the capers, mustard, and lemon juice in a bowl. Stir in the herbs and the olive oil and season the dressing to taste with salt. Set aside.

Meanwhile, bring a large pot of water to a boil and add the sweet potatoes, beets, and a large pinch of salt. Cook until the vegetables are very tender, about 20 minutes. Drain the vegetables and place them back in the empty pot. Use a potato masher to crush them. Season the mash to taste with salt and place it on a serving platter.

Place the butter and thyme in a large, heavy skillet set over medium-high heat. Once it starts to turn a bit brown, add the scallops to the pan and season them with salt. Cook until well browned on the bottom, 2–3 minutes at the most, and then turn them and cook until just browned on the other side, another 2 minutes. Remove the pan from the heat and discard the thyme.

Arrange the scallops on the mash and drizzle over whatever browned butter is left in the pan. Drizzle the caper salsa verde over the scallops, garnish the dish with a few dollops of crème fraîche, and scatter with a few greens or chopped parsley,

CURRIED BLACK LENTILS + ROASTED CAULIFLOWER

We served this dish when we briefly had a pop-up restaurant in Paris. We got off the plane without a plan, so we went straight to the market. It was quite early in the morning and we had barely slept and, as it turned out, the vendors at the market were already tipsy. They fed us cheese and some of their wine and all of a sudden, we loved France. We wrote the entire menu for the pop-up at the market and this dish was a favorite of the evening—a magic combination of great French lentils, gorgeous cauliflower, and bacchanal inspiration.

Serves 6

¼ cup olive oil, divided
½ a yellow onion, thinly sliced
2 tablespoons red curry paste (or Vindaloo Paste from page 146)
1 large tomato, stem discarded, diced
1 cup black lentils, soaked overnight in cold water and drained
2 cups vegetable stock
Coarse salt and freshly ground black pepper
6 cups cauliflower florets
2 tablespoons butter
2 sprigs thyme
1 cup plain yogurt for serving (preferably sheep's milk)
2 tablespoons roughly chopped cilantro

Place 2 tablespoons of olive oil in a large pot set over medium-high heat and add the onion. Cook, stirring now and then, until softened and browned, about 10 minutes. Add the curry paste, tomato, and lentils and stir to combine. Pour in the vegetable stock and bring the mixture to a boil. Lower the heat and simmer, stirring now and then, until the lentils are just softened, about half an hour. Season to taste with salt and set aside.

Meanwhile, heat 2 more tablespoons of olive oil in a separate large pot set over medium-high heat. Add the cauliflower florets to the pot and cook, stirring now and then, until browned in spots, 10 minutes. Add the butter, thyme, and ½ cup of water. Turn the heat to low and cover. Cook until the cauliflower is tender, 10 minutes. Uncover the pot, discard the thyme, and season to taste with more salt and pepper if necessary.

To serve, place the lentils to a serving platter and arrange the cauliflower on top. Dollop the yogurt over the cauliflower, scatter with the cilantro, and serve immediately.

FAT RADISH PLATE: GINGER BROWN RICE, STEAMED KABOCHA + KALE + CIPPOLINI ONIONS, ADZUKI BEANS WITH BARLEY MISO, CARROTS + HIJIKI WITH ALMONDS, PICKLED VEGETABLES, CARROT-GINGER PUREE, TAHINI DRESSING

This uber-healthy plate of many components, each quite simple to prepare, is completely inspired by Charles Holdsworth-Hunt, Ben's stepfather. Charles is one of England's most well-respected macrobiotic chefs and teachers. He helped us create this dish for the restaurant. One of our best-selling dishes, it's our homage to great food and health and, of course, him.

Serves 8

2 cups brown rice, rinsed
1 (2-inch) knob of ginger, peeled and grated
1 teaspoon coarse salt
1 kabocha squash, seeded and cut into wedges
Leaves from 1 bunch of kale
1½ dozen cippolini onions, peeled
Adzuki Beans with Barley Miso (see page 158)
Carrots + Hijiki with Almonds (see page 158)
Cider-Braised Red Cabbage (see page 213)
Pickled Vegetables (see page 161)
Carrot-Ginger Purée (see page 161)
Tahini Dressing (see page 161)
White and black sesame seeds

Place the rice, ginger, and salt in a saucepot and add 3½ cups of water. Bring the mixture to a boil, lower the heat, cover the pot, and cook until the rice is tender, about 45 minutes. Keep the rice covered and set it aside.

In a bamboo steamer, cook the squash, kale, and onions until they're tender. Set aside.

To serve, evenly divide the rice between 8 shallow bowls or plates and evenly divide the steamed vegetables between them. Add a spoonful of the Adzuki Beans with Barley Miso, the Carrots + Hijiki with Almonds, the Cider-Braised Red Cabbage, and the Pickled Vegetables. Serve with bowls of Carrot-Ginger Puree and Tahini Dressing and a small bowl of black and white sesame seeds.

ADZUKI BEANS WITH BARLEY MISO

1 cup dry adzuki beans, soaked overnight in cold water, drained
1 medium carrot, halved crosswise
1 celery stalk, halved crosswise
1 small onion, halved crosswise
1 bay leaf
2 tablespoons barley miso
Coarse salt

Place the drained beans in a large pot along with the carrot, celery, onion, bay leaf, and miso. Cover with water and bring the mixture to a boil. Lower the heat and simmer until the beans are tender, about an hour. Drain the beans, discard the vegetables and bay leaf, and season the beans to taste with salt. Serve warm.

CARROTS + HIJIKI WITH ALMONDS

½ cup dried hijiki (1 ounce)
2 carrots (preferably different colors, but okay if not), scrubbed and
  roughly chopped
1 tablespoon soy sauce
½ cup toasted almonds, roughly chopped
Coarse salt

Place the hijiki in a small bowl and cover with warm water. Soak for 15 minutes.

Place the hijiki, its soaking liquid, and the carrots in a large skillet and pour over enough extra water to nearly cover the carrots. Bring the mixture to a boil, lower the heat, and simmer until the carrots are soft and nearly all of the cooking liquid is evaporated, about 15 minutes. Stir in the soy sauce and scatter over the almonds. Season to taste with salt and serve warm or at room temperature.

lunch + dinner

PICKLED VEGETABLES

1 cucumber, thinly sliced
1 bunch red radishes, thinly sliced
2 tablespoons umeboshi vinegar

Place the cucumber and radish slices in a bowl. Sprinkle the vegetables with the vinegar and place a plate on top to weigh them down. Place something heavy (like a can) on top of the plate and allow the pickles to sit for an hour. Drain off the liquid before serving.

CARROT-GINGER PURÉE

Makes 2 cups

4 carrots, peeled and thinly sliced
1 (2 inch) knob ginger, peeled and minced
1½ cups vegetable stock
2 tablespoons toasted sesame oil
½ cup olive oil

Place the carrots, ginger, and stock in a medium pot set over high heat. Bring to a boil, lower the heat and simmer until the carrots are tender, about 10 minutes. Transfer the contents of the pot to a blender, add the oils, and puree until smooth. Season the dressing to taste with salt and pepper.

TAHINI DRESSING
½ cup water
2 tablespoons honey
1 tablespoon toasted sesame oil
1 tablespoon soy sauce
2 tablespoons freshly squeezed lemon juice
½ cup tahini paste
½ teaspoon coarse salt

Combine all of the ingredients in a blender and puree until smooth.

This page: Director of operations Adam Wright-Smith and Phil enjoy a wine break while shooting the book. Opposite page, left to right: Roast chicken ready for its close-up. Sitting down for a Sunday roast—there is nothing better.

PUMPKIN MERINGUE PIE

This is a great, impressive alternative to the classic preparation of pumpkin pie.

Makes 1 pie

1 store-bought or homemade pastry shell
¾ cup light brown sugar
½ teaspoon salt
1 teaspoon ground cinnamon
½ teaspoon ground ginger
¼ teaspoon ground cloves
1 (15-ounce) can unsweetened pumpkin purée
2 whole eggs, beaten
¾ cup whole milk
¾ cup heavy cream
4 egg whites
½ cup superfine sugar

Preheat oven to 425°F.

Line a pie tin with the pastry and set it aside.

In a large bowl, whisk together the brown sugar, salt, spices, pumpkin, eggs, milk, and cream until completely smooth. Pour into the pastry shell and bake for 15 minutes. Reduce the heat to 350°F and bake until a knife inserted in center of pie comes out clean, an additional 40–45 minutes. Remove the pie from the oven and allow it to cool completely.

Preheat the broiler.

Combine the eggs whites and sugar in a mixing bowl set over a pot of simmering water, being sure the water doesn't touch the bowl. Stir until the sugar completely dissolves into the egg whites and then remove the bowl from the pot. Place the mixture in the bowl of a stand mixer (or use a hand mixer) and beat until glossy, stiff peaks form, about 5 minutes.

Pile the meringue on top of the pumpkin pie and broil until the meringue is browned like a toasted marshmallow, just a minute. Slice and serve!

WINTER

FULL ENGLISH BREAKFAST

This is the ultimate breakfast and is especially great for hangovers, which, let's be honest, we all have now and then.

Serves 4

2 large tomatoes, quartered
Fresh thyme sprigs
Olive oil
Coarse salt and freshly ground black pepper
A large bunch of mushrooms (whatever type you like), thickly sliced
8 strips bacon
8 chipolata sausages (or your favorite breakfast sausages)
8 eggs
1 (13.5-ounce) can Heinz baked beans
4 thick slices toasted sourdough bread

Preheat oven to 400°F.

Place the tomatoes on a baking sheet with a few sprigs of thyme. Drizzle with 2 tablespoons of olive oil and season with salt and pepper. Roast the tomatoes, stirring now and then, until softened and a bit browned, about 20 minutes. Remove the tomatoes from the oven and set aside.

Meanwhile, heat 2 tablespoons of olive oil in a large skillet and add the mushrooms and another couple of sprigs of thyme. Cook, stirring a bit, until browned all over and softened, about 10 minutes. Season the mushrooms to taste with salt and pepper and set them aside.

Place the bacon and the sausages in a large skillet set over medium-high heat and cook, turning them now and then, until browned and crispy, about 10 minutes. Set aside.

Cook the eggs however you like them!

Warm the beans in a small pot.

To serve, evenly divide all the components onto four plates and DIG IN.

BRUSSELS SPROUT BUBBLE + SQUEAK

Bubble and squeak is an old-fashioned British dish that typically consists of the leftover potatoes and cabbage from a Sunday night roast (the name comes from the noise the vegetables make when you heat them up). Combining potatoes with Brussels sprouts and bacon, we love this seasonal, slightly Yankee take on an old English favorite. Served with poached eggs, it's the perfect brunch dish.

Serves 4

1 baking potato, diced
1 pound Brussels sprouts, quartered lengthwise
½ pound thick cut bacon, sliced into bite-sized pieces
1 yellow onion, thinly sliced
Coarse salt and freshly ground black pepper
4 poached eggs
Small handful chopped chives

Bring a large pot of water to a boil and add the potatoes. Cook until just tender, about 15 minutes. Using a slotted spoon, transfer the potatoes to a paper towel-lined plate and set them aside. Place the Brussels sprouts in the water and cook until they're just tender, about 5 minutes. Transfer them to the same plate with the potatoes.

Meanwhile, place the bacon in a large, heavy skillet set over medium-high heat. Cook, stirring now and then, until the fat is rendered and the bacon is crisp, about 6 minutes. Using a slotted spoon, transfer the bacon to a plate and set it aside. Add the onion to the skillet and cook, stirring now and then, until beginning to soften, about 10 minutes. Add the reserved potatoes and Brussels sprouts to the onions and cook until everything is very well browned and cooked through, another 10–15 minutes. Return the crisp bacon to the pan and stir to combine everything. Season the mixture to taste with salt and pepper.

Transfer the vegetable mixture to 4 plates. Top each serving with one egg and scatter generously with chives. Serve immediately.

BANANA BREAD

When we started off as caterers, the arrangement for our commercial kitchen meant we only had access to it from eight at night until six in the morning. All of our friends started thinking we were so great because we had warm, fresh banana bread around. The truth is we were just up all night and it was always the last thing we made! Feel free to add a cup of chopped nuts, dried fruit (chopped apricots, dates, prunes, or raisins), or chocolate chips to this basic recipe. Serve with plenty of soft, salted butter.

Makes one 9-inch loaf

6 tablespoons butter, at room temperature, plus a little extra for the pan
⅔ cup sugar
1 egg, beaten
1 teaspoon vanilla extract
1¾ cups all-purpose flour, plus extra for the pan
2 teaspoons baking powder
¼ teaspoon baking soda
½ teaspoon salt
3 very ripe bananas, mashed
1 cup chopped nuts, dried fruit, or chocolate chips (optional)

Preheat oven to 350°F. Coat a 9"x5"x13" loaf pan with a little butter and dust with flour.

In a large bowl, stir together the 6 tablespoons of butter, sugar, and eggs until very creamy. In a separate bowl, sift the flour, baking powder, baking soda, and salt together. Little by little, add the sifted ingredients to the butter mixture alternating with the mashed banana, beating the batter smooth with each addition. At this point, fold in any of the optional ingredients if you're using them. Place the batter in the prepared loaf pan.

Bake the bread until browned and the center springs back when lightly pressed with your fingertip, about 1 hour.

Cool the loaf in the pan for 10 minutes before turning onto a wire rack to cool completely.

KALE CAESAR SALAD

We founded Silkstone, our catering company, before kale became popular. At the time, it was a weird vegetable with a bad association, and our slogan, seriously, was "kale is sexy." We've always thought of kale as the cool, misunderstood kid at school who all of sudden shows up at the reunion and is a rock star.

Serves 4

Dressing
4 anchovy filets
1 egg yolk
1 teaspoon Dijon mustard
¼ cup grated Parmesan cheese
Pinch dried oregano
Zest and juice of ½ lemon
2 tablespoons olive oil
¼ cup canola oil
Coarse salt and freshly ground black pepper

Salad
Leaves from a bunch of curly kale, torn into bite-sized pieces (6 cups)
Juice from half a lemon
4 pieces crispy bacon, coarsely chopped
2 Six-Minute Eggs (see page 68), peeled and quartered
1 cup croutons

For the dressing, place the anchovies, egg yolk, mustard, Parmesan, oregano, lemon zest and juice, and 2 tablespoons of water in a food processor and pulse until well blended. With the machine running, slowly drizzle in the oils to form an emulsified dressing. Season to taste with salt and pepper. Set the dressing aside.

Place the kale in a large bowl and pour over the lemon juice. Using your hands, massage the kale together with the lemon juice to help it soften. Pour over the dressing and toss to combine. Place the dressed kale on a serving platter or on individual salad plates and scatter with the bacon, eggs, and croutons. Serve immediately.

BEET AND SWISS CHARD CRUMBLE

There's a beloved restaurant in Portland, Oregon called Paley's Place and they have a wonderful cookbook that features a number of savory crumbles. Inspired by those, we developed this one that is full of beets, greens, a nutty topping, and a rich, cheesy béchamel sauce. It makes any dinner very special.

Makes 1 large crumble

2 cups flour, divided
½ cup oats
½ cup finely chopped toasted hazelnuts
Pinch grated nutmeg
Coarse salt and freshly ground black pepper
2 sticks unsalted butter, cold and diced, divided
4½ cups coarsely grated clothbound cheddar cheese, divided
4 pounds beets, peeled and chopped
Small handful thyme sprigs
4 garlic cloves, crushed
½ teaspoon black peppercorns
1 bunch Swiss chard, roughly chopped
4 cups milk
¼ cup English mustard
Tabasco sauce

In a large bowl, mix together 1 cup of the flour with the oats, hazelnuts, nutmeg, and a pinch each of salt and pepper. Using your fingertips, work in 1 stick of the butter and ½ cup of the cheddar until the mixture turns into coarse crumbs. Set the mixture aside.

Bring a large pot of salted water to a boil and add the beets, thyme, garlic, and black peppercorns. Cook until the beets are just tender, about 10–15 minutes. Drain the beets (discarding the thyme, garlic, and peppercorns) and set them aside.

Place the remaining stick of butter in a saucepot set over medium-low heat. Once it melts, stir in the remaining cup of flour and cook until the mixture smells cooked but doesn't take on any color, about 5–10 minutes. While stirring, slowly pour in the milk. Bring the mixture to a boil, lower the heat, and cook until a thick sauce forms, about 5 minutes. Stir in the remaining 4 cups of cheese and the mustard. Season the sauce to taste with Tabasco, salt, and pepper. Keep warm over a low flame.

Preheat the oven to 350°F.

Spread a third of the cheese sauce on the bottom of a buttered 9"x13" baking dish. Top with a third of the beets and Swiss chard. Season the vegetables with salt and pepper. Repeat the process two more times and then cover the entire surface with crumble topping.

Bake until the filling is bubbling and top is crisp and browned, about 50 minutes. Serve hot.

ROOT VEG STACK

We made this as part of our first catering dinner at Silkstone, which was cooked out of the apartment we shared. The morning after the dinner, we woke up late and realized we had to man a table at a food business expo that day and had nothing to bring. We cut up the leftovers from the Root Veg Stack, bought some toothpicks, and ran over. A super important lady came up to our table, took a bite, and said, "I want you in my office next Monday." The next thing we knew, we were presenting to all of the event planners for a major American corporation on the top of an NYC skyscraper about current trends in catering. We barely knew how to use PowerPoint! This is all to say that you should never underestimate the possibility of leftovers.

Serves 8

1 cup heavy cream
2 ½ pounds root vegetables, peeled (we love a mix of baking potatoes,
    sweet potatoes, carrots, parsnips, and golden beets)
Coarse salt and freshly ground black pepper

Preheat the oven to 375°F. Line an 8-inch square baking dish with parchment paper and set it aside.

Place the cream in a small saucepan and bring to a boil. Lower the heat and simmer until the cream is reduced by half, about 15 minutes. Set the cream aside to cool.

Meanwhile, using a mandoline, carefully slice the root vegetables lengthwise into very thin slices. Lay down a single layer of the root vegetables, slightly overlapping each piece, and then season the layer with salt and pepper. Drizzle 2 tablespoons of the reduced cream over the layer. Repeat the process, layering over and over again until you've used up all of the root vegetables and the cream. Place a piece of parchment paper over the top of the dish and then place another baking dish on top of the root vegetables so that it weighs the vegetables down.

Carefully place the baking dishes into the oven and bake until the vegetables are tender, 1 hour. Carefully remove the baking dishes from the oven and allow the root vegetables to cool to room temperature. Place the baking dishes on top of a sheet pan and place the whole thing in the refrigerator overnight to cool. (The baking sheet will catch any liquid that comes over the edges.)

The next day, heat the oven back to 375°F. Invert the vegetable stack onto a cutting board and cut it into large serving pieces. Transfer the pieces to a parchment-lined baking sheet and warm the pieces in the oven for 10 minutes and then serve immediately.

This pressing down, cooling, and reheating will give you gorgeous, compressed layers. Alternatively, you can serve the root vegetables straight from the pan right after the first baking. It won't be as beautiful, but it will surely be delicious.

GRILLED CHEESE SANDWICHES WITH HOMEMADE BRANSTON PICKLE

In the UK, everyone grows up eating cheese with Branston pickle, a sort of pickled chutney that's full of different vegetables and spices. The actual recipe is top secret, but we developed a version that's as close to the jar as we could get. Of course, if you don't feel like making it, the jarred version will do (if you can't find Branston pickle, just substitute any great chutney). Serve these sandwiches with slices of Homemade Pickles (see page 104) for a double dose of pickles!

Makes a single sandwich, easily multiplied

2 tablespoons Homemade Branston Pickle
2 slices crusty sourdough bread
½ cup grated clothbound cheddar cheese
1 tablespoon softened butter

Place the Homemade Branston Pickle in a food processor and process until smooth. Spread the smooth mixture on one slice of bread and top with the cheese. Place the second slice of bread on top. Butter the outside of both sides of the sandwich and place it in a frying pan set over medium heat. Cook the sandwich, flipping once, until golden brown on both sides and the cheese is melted, about 5 minutes. Serve immediately.

HOMEMADE BRANSTON PICKLE

Makes 4 cups

1 small carrot, peeled and finely diced
1 small rutabaga (about ½ pound), peeled and finely diced
3 garlic cloves, minced
½ cup dates, pitted and finely chopped
2 cups cauliflower florets, finely chopped
1 yellow onion, finely diced
1 zucchini, finely diced
1 dozen cornichons, finely chopped
¾ cup dark brown sugar
½ teaspoon coarse salt
2 tablespoons freshly squeezed lemon juice
¾ cup malt vinegar
1 teaspoon mustard seeds

Stir together all the ingredients in a large saucepan and add a cup of water. Set the pot over high heat and bring to a boil. Turn the heat to low and simmer, stirring now and then, until thickened and all the vegetables are softened, about 1½ hours.

DUCK CONFIT TERRINE WITH RED ONION JAM

A terrine sounds like a complicated thing, but really it's easy to do. It's just a matter of packing a terrine mold (or a loaf pan) quite full and weighting it down. We make our own duck confit for this—something also that sounds complicated, but couldn't be easier   but feel free to buy duck confit and go from there. This is amazing served with thick slices of toast, red onion jam, and plenty of mustard.

Makes one 2-quart terrine (serves 12)

2 tablespoons coriander seeds
2 tablespoons fennel seeds
3 tablespoons whole black peppercorns
1 pound coarse salt
1 cup brown sugar
3 bay leaves
2 whole oranges, halved
6 Muscovy duck legs
2 quarts duck fat, at room temperature
2 heads of garlic, halved horizontally
4 sprigs rosemary
8 sprigs thyme
1 egg
2 tablespoons whole grain mustard
2 tablespoons sherry vinegar
1 cup finely chopped parsley
Freshly ground black pepper
Red Onion Jam, for serving

Place the coriander and fennel seeds in a skillet set over medium heat and cook, stirring, until they're aromatic, about 1 minute. Transfer the seeds to a mortar along with the black peppercorns. Crush with a pestle and transfer the spices to a large bowl. Add the salt, sugar, and bay leaves. Squeeze the juice from the oranges into the bowl, stir to combine, and then toss in the spent orange halves.

Place half of the salt mixture in the bottom of a large baking dish. Place the duck legs, skin side up, on top of the salt, and place the remaining half of the salt mixture on top. Cover the dish with plastic wrap and place it in the refrigerator overnight to cure the duck.

COLORADO LAMB + ROOT VEGETABLE STEW

England loves a stew, and whenever we go back home, our moms are always serving them. You don't see stews too much on restaurant menus because they're such a homey thing, and we love serving them to guests for just that reason. Nick is from Colorado, where some of the best lamb in the States is from, and he came up with this simple stew that also includes plenty of hearty vegetables.

Serves 4

1 pound boneless lamb shoulder, cut into 1-inch pieces (or buy cubed stew meat)
Coarse salt and freshly ground black pepper
Flour for dredging
Olive oil
1 cup pearl onions, peeled (or 1 red onion, diced)
3 garlic cloves, smashed
½ teaspoon ground cumin
2 tablespoons tomato paste
2½ cups chicken stock, divided
1 large potato, cut lengthwise into thick wedges
2 carrots, peeled and cut into large pieces
2 parsnips, peeled and cut into large pieces
1 bunch kale, leaves roughly chopped

Season the lamb meat aggressively with salt and pepper and lightly dredge with flour.

Place 3 tablespoons of olive oil in a large soup pot set over medium-high heat. Place the meat in the pot and cook, turning the pieces now and then, until browned all over, about 10 minutes. Add the onions, garlic, cumin, and tomato paste to the meat and stir to combine. Add 1½ cups of the chicken stock and bring the mixture to a boil. Turn the heat to low and simmer the stew until the meat is tender, about 1 hour.

Meanwhile, heat another 3 tablespoons of oil in another large pot set over medium-high heat. Add the potato, carrots, and parsnips and cook, stirring now and then, until browned in spots, about 10 minutes. Add the remaining cup of chicken stock to the pot and season the vegetables with salt and pepper. Turn the heat to low, cover the pot, and simmer until the vegetables are tender, about 20 minutes.

Stir the cooked root vegetables into the tender lamb and then fold in the kale. Cook until the kale is wilted, a final 5 minutes. Serve hot!

COTTAGE PIE

Shepherd's pie is all about lamb (shepherds flock sheep after all!). While we love lamb, we're even bigger fans of cottage pie. To be honest, we're not really sure what cottages have to do with cows, but nevertheless we love the classic combination of flavorful minced beef topped with rich mashed potatoes.

Serves 4

Coarse salt
3 baking potatoes, peeled and cut into 1-inch pieces
4 tablespoons butter
1 cup cream
3 tablespoons olive oil
1 pound ground beef
Freshly ground black pepper
1 carrot, peeled and finely diced
1 celery stalk, finely diced
1 yellow onion, finely diced
1 bay leaf
1 teaspoon minced thyme
½ cup dry red wine
1 (15-ounce) can diced tomatoes

Preheat oven to 425°F.

Bring a large pot of salted water to a boil and add the potatoes. Boil until the potatoes are very tender, about 25 minutes. Drain the potatoes and return them to the pot. Add the butter and cream, then mash with a potato masher. Season the mash to taste with salt and set aside.

Meanwhile, place the oil in a large cast-iron skillet set over medium-high heat. Add the beef and season with a large pinch of salt and a few grinds of black pepper. Cook the beef, stirring now and then, until browned, about 15 minutes. Using a slotted spoon, transfer the meat to a bowl and set it aside. Place the carrots, celery, onion, bay leaf, and thyme in the skillet and cook until the vegetables are softened and a bit browned, about 15 minutes. Return the beef to the skillet and add the wine and the tomatoes. Bring the mixture to a boil, lower the heat to a simmer, and cook until the mixture is happy, about 15 minutes. Season to taste with salt and pepper.

Spread the mash on top of the meat mixture and transfer the skillet to the oven. Bake until the top is a bit browned, about 15 minutes. Serve immediately.

DEVILED BRUSSELS SPROUTS

Our version of Devils on Horseback (bacon-wrapped prunes stuffed with blue cheese), this party snack balances the sweetness of glazed Brussels sprouts with hot chili and salty, smoky bacon. To make these devils vegetarian, simply omit the bacon.

Makes 3 dozen

1 ½ cups apple cider
¾ cup cranberry juice
½ teaspoon chili flakes
2 teaspoons sweet chili sauce
3 dozen Brussels sprouts, stem ends trimmed
18 strips bacon, cut in half crosswise

Preheat the oven to 350°F. Line a baking sheet with parchment paper and set it aside.

Place the apple cider, cranberry juice, chili flakes, and chili sauce in a small pot set over high heat. Bring to a boil, lower the heat to medium, and continue to boil until the mixture is reduced by half, about 15 minutes. Set the mixture aside to cool.

Meanwhile, bring a large pot of water to a boil and add the sprouts. Cook until just tender, about 10 minutes. Drain the sprouts and rinse them with cool water to keep them from overcooking. Pat them dry with paper towels and then wrap each one with half a strip of bacon. Place the wrapped sprouts on the prepared baking sheet. Pour ⅔ of the glaze over the sprouts being sure to get some on each sprout. Place the sprouts in the oven and roast until golden brown, about 20 minutes. Remove the sprouts from the oven and pour over the final ⅓ of the glaze. Return the sprouts to the oven for a final 10 minutes just to get that last bit of glaze to hold really tight. Serve hot.

ROAST BEEF + CRISPY POTATOES

The beef fat is the star of this roast—it flavors not only the potatoes, but the Yorkshire Puddings, too. Serve with mustard, Sautéed Greens, and Cider-Braised Red Cabbage (page 213), and some mashed acorn squash (just use a fork to mash steamed or roasted squash with plenty of butter and season with salt).

Serves 8

2 pounds small creamer potatoes, peeled
1 (3-pound) beef roast, trimmed of excess fat
Coarse salt and freshly ground black pepper
2 tablespoons olive oil
A few sprigs rosemary

Preheat your oven to 375°F.

Bring a large pot of water to a boil and add the potatoes. Cook until just beginning to get tender, about 10 minutes. Drain the potatoes, place them back in the empty pot, and cover. Holding the lid down and the handles of the pot at the same time, aggressively shake the potatoes so that the surface area of the potatoes gets a bit shaggy. Set the potatoes aside.

Season the beef generously with salt and pepper.

Heat 2 tablespoons the oil in a large cast iron skillet over medium-high heat until very hot but not smoking. Add the meat and sear on all sides.

Put the skillet in the oven and roast until an instant-read thermometer registers 130°F, about 40 minutes. Transfer the roast to a cutting board and tent with a piece of foil while you finish the potatoes.

Remove ¼ cup of fat from the pan and reserve it for the Yorkshire Puddings.

Place the potatoes in the rest of the fat and season generously with salt and pepper. Scatter over the rosemary sprigs and return the skillet to the oven. Roast, shaking the pan every so often, until the potatoes are browned and crispy, about 25 minutes. Slice the beef and serve with the potatoes.

YORKSHIRE PUDDINGS

A staple of traditional Sunday roasts in England, Yorkshire pudding isn't a pudding by American standards—it's much more like a popover. Devised as a way to use the leftover fat from the roast beef, the puddings, quite magically, puff up in the hot grease.

Makes 10

4 eggs
1 cup milk
1 cup flour
½ teaspoon salt
¼ cup fat from roast beef (or butter or shortening)

Preheat the oven to 450°F.

In a medium bowl, whisk the eggs and milk together until they're really foamy. Stir in the flour and salt.

Meanwhile, divide the fat (or butter or shortening) between 10 muffin cups in a standard tin and place it in the oven to heat until really hot, at least 10 minutes.

Quickly take the tray out of the oven and divide the batter between the cups. Return it to the oven and cook until puffed and brown and dry, about 15 minutes. Serve immediately.

CIDER-BRAISED RED CABBAGE

We also use this cabbage in a very different kind of feast, as part of our
vegetarian Fat Radish Plate (page 157).

Serves 8

1 small head red cabbage, core discarded, thinly sliced
1 green apple, peeled, seeded, and thinly sliced
1 small red onion, peeled and thinly sliced
2 cups apple cider
Apple cider vinegar
Coarse salt

Place the cabbage, apple, onion, and apple cider in a large pot set over high
heat. Bring to a boil, lower the heat, and simmer, stirring now and then, until the
cabbage is totally soft and succulent, about an hour. Season the cabbage with
vinegar and salt before serving.

SAUTÉED GREENS

Use any particular type of green you'd like here (kale, collards, Swiss chard, bok
choy, spinach, etc.) or a combination of a few.

Serves 8

¼ cup olive oil
3 garlic cloves, thinly sliced
½ teaspoon red chili flakes
3 pounds hearty greens, roughly chopped
½ cup vegetable stock
Coarse salt

Place the olive oil in a large pot set over medium-high heat. Add the garlic and
chili flakes and cook until fragrant, just a minute. Add the greens and the
stock and stir to combine with the garlicky oil. Cover the pot and cook until the
greens are tender, about 5 minutes. Uncover and continue to cook, stirring,
until all of the liquid is evaporated, 5 minutes. Season the greens to taste with
salt and serve immediately.

BANOFFEE PIE

Banoffee pie is basically what happens when a banana bumps into toffee and then, together, they collide with a chocolate pastry crust and clouds of whipped cream. As the story goes, it was invented in a pub in Sussex called The Hungry Monk in 1972. We fell in love with it at home in England and, luckily, our American customers love it too.

Makes 1 pie

Crust
8 tablespoons unsalted butter, at room temperature
¼ cup icing sugar
2 egg yolks
½ teaspoon vanilla extract
1 cup flour
¼ cup cocoa powder
¼ teaspoon salt

Filling
½ cup sugar
4 tablespoons unsalted butter
1 (14-ounce) can sweetened condensed milk

Assembly
3 ripe bananas, peeled and sliced
2 cups heavy cream, whipped
½ cup coarsely grated dark chocolate

For the crust, place the butter and icing sugar into the bowl of a stand mixer and beat until fluffy. Beat in the egg yolks and the vanilla extract. Fold in the flour, cocoa powder, and salt. Press the dough into a pie pan. Prick the surface all over with a fork and refrigerate it for 30 minutes.

Bake the crust in a 350°F oven until it's firm to the touch, about 20 minutes. Cool to room temperature.

While the crust is cooling, place the filling ingredients into a saucepan and bring to a boil. Lower the heat and simmer, stirring now and then, until the mixture forms a thick caramel, about 20 minutes. Pour the filling into the tart crust and let it cool to room temperature. Top with the sliced bananas, spread the whipped cream over the bananas, and finish with the grated chocolate. Refrigerate the pie for at least an hour before slicing and serving.

This page, left to right: Baby beets for a warm winter salad. Essential tools. Opposite page: Team photo. How lucky we are to work with such talented and passionate people.

Index

Index

Index

acknowledgments

So many incredible people have helped us make the Fat Radish what it is, and joined us in the adventure of creating this book.

Our incredible team at Fat Radish HQ, past and present: You are like family and we feel so lucky to work with such a passionate and talented group of people.

Nicholas Wilber: You are the calmest, hardest working, most knowledgeable, and talented chef out there, and you have been integral to the success of our restaurants. It has been such a pleasure to watch you grow with the farm-to-table movement, of which you've been such a strong advocate and pioneer.

Julia Turshen: A total rock star and a pretty big deal, but to us you're still the girl with the big hair and chucks who gave lessons to the team on raw food. Your journey is so inspiring and fitting for this book and we've been lucky to work with you. You listened to the stories, and acted as a mediator when we fought about which ones to include.

Thanks to Adam Wright-Smith, our amazing operations manager; our dear friend and land-lord, Trevor Stahelski, who gave two boys a chance when we had the idea for the Fat Radish; Jos and Annabel White, whose support and friendship allowed our vision come to life; Allie Pyke—you are so much more to the restaurant than just a partner; Tom Clift, for believing in us and helping get the Radish off the ground; Oberon Sinclair, for intro-ducing us to Rizzoli and making this book happen; Caitlin Leffel, our incredible editor at Rizzoli, for guiding us through the process of creating this book, not an easy task!; Erika Oliveira, our amazing book designer; Nicole Franzen (aka 'Franzzini"), for working with such amateurs like us. All your patience and hard work shows in your beautiful photos; Kate Deez, for capturing so many adventures and for letting us steal your handwriting; and to our dear friends, Ben Pundole, Alexander and Misha Gilkes, Carl and Maud Heline, Joe Termini, Jamie Mcdonald, Peter Semple, and Tess, Tom, and Anthony Martignetti, Tommy Mendez, Helen Rockefeller Armide, our Brazilian family (Mauricio, Felipe, and Antonio), Morten Sandtroen, and Andy Plume.

Peter Gladwin, thank you for igniting Phil's passion for food and farming, and Richard Gladwin, thanks for helping us start the adventure seven years ago; thank you Sidgwick family for the fun we had growing up at your beautiful farm in England.

Mickey Sumner, Trudie Styler, and Sting, thanks for being true visionaries of organic farming and food, and for your support and friendship; thanks to Jim Denevan and the Outstanding in the Field team, Patrick Martins, and Anne Saxelby for being so inspiring and supportive.

And to our wonderful families: Nigel, Shane, Kate Winser, Susie, Charlie Boy, Zander, Alice, Josh, Raffie, Rosie, Charlie, Poppy, and Teddy.

We could not do what we do without daily support from our amazing ladies—Kate Deez and Dree. You and your families have embraced us and helped us through so much, par-ticularly through the writing of this book.

Ben & Phil

First published in the United States in 2014 by
Rizzoli International Publications, Inc.
300 Park Avenue South
New York, NY 10010
www.rizzoliusa.com

Designed by Erika Oliveira
Text by Julia Turshen
Photographs by Nicole Franzen
Edited by Caitlin Leffel

© 2014 Ben Towill and Phil Winser
Photographs on pages 88–89, 112–113, 128–129
and 149 by Kate Deez
Photographs on pages 87 and 98–99 by
Emily Johnston
Cover image styled by Kate Jordan (props) and
Chelsea Zimmer (food)

ISBN: 978-0-8478-4334-3
Library of Congress Number: 2014934108

2014 2015 2016 2017
10 9 8 7 6 5 4 3 2 1

Printed in China